The Downshifters' Guide to Relocation

If you want to know how ...

Seven Steps to Leaving the Rat Race
Freeing yourself from the 9–5 grind

Returning to Education
A practical handbook for adult learners

Build Your Own Home
The ultimate guide to managing a self-build project and creating your dream house

Tracking Down Your Ancestors
Discover the story behind your ancestors and bring your family history to life

7 Ways to Beat the Pension Crisis

howtobooks

Please send for a free copy of the latest catalogue to:
How To Books
3 Newtec Place, Magdalen Road
Oxford OX4 1RE, United Kingdom
Email: info@howtobooks.co.uk
www.howtobooks.co.uk

The Downshifters' Guide to Relocation

Chris and Gillean Sangster

 **howto**books

Published by How To Books Ltd,
3 Newtec Place, Magdalen Road,
Oxford OX4 1RE. United Kingdom.
Tel: (01865) 793806. Fax: (01865) 248780
email: info@howtobooks.co.uk
www.howtobooks.co.uk

British Library Cataloguing in Publication Data.
A catalogue record for this book is available from the British Library.

Produced for How To Books by Deer Park Productions, Tavistock
Cover design by Baseline Arts Ltd, Oxford
Photographs in text by Kate Bailey, John Duggan and Tom Fryer

Typesetting and design by Sparks – www.sparks.co.uk
Printed and bound in Great Britain by Bell & Bain Ltd, Glasgow

NOTE: The material contained in this book is set out in good faith for general
guidance and no liability can be accepted for loss or expense incurred as a result
of relying in particular circumstances on statements made in this book. Laws and
regulations are complex and liable to change, and readers should check the current
position with the relevant authorities before making personal arrangements.

Contents

Preface   *xi*

1 Relocation and downshifting: introduction   1
What's the plan?   2
Work/life balance   2
Downshifting and relocation   3
Reality check   6
The range of our investigations   8

Part One: Deciding whether downshifting and relocation is right for you   9

2 Are you ready?   11
Why do you want to downshift?   11
Action plan 2.1   14
What kind of person are you?   14
Action plan 2.2   17
Changing direction   18
Action Plan 2.3   20
Moving forward   21

3 Deciding what's best for you — 22
Carrying out a SWOT analysis — 23
Action plan 3.1 — 24
The options open to you — 25
Being objective — 26
Having a 'Blue Water' — 27
Case study — 28
Action plan 3.2 — 28
Choosing your skills — 29
Action plan 3.3 — 30
Review time — 31
When 'what' becomes 'where' — 31
Check point: Action plan 3.1 — 32

4 Choosing your location — 33
Commuting territory — 33
Transport — 41
What next? — 42

5 What type of property? — 43
Consolidating your thoughts — 43
Hotels, guest houses, B & Bs — 43
Self-catering — 46
Pottery, painting, sculpture workshops — 47
Shop or gallery — 48
Farms, market gardens, stables, outdoor centres, etc. — 49
House with an office — 50
Action plan 5.1 — 51
Some real property considerations — 52
To sum up — 53

6 Balancing your life and work — 55
Action plan 6.1 — 56
The 24/7 world of self-employment — 57
Effective working: an attitude of mind — 59

Differing balance points   60
Flexibility and selectivity   61
Action plan 6.2   63

7 *The story so far*   **65**
Where do I stand?   65
Action plan 7.1   66
Action plan 7.2   67
Applying SWOT   67
Action plan 7.3   67
Inspiration   68
The next stage   69
Action plan 7.4   70
Choosing your new location   71
Action plan 7.5   72
Out of the mists of confusion   73
Action plan 7.6   74

■ **Part Two: Establishing details and realities**   **75**

8 *Property matters: getting the calculations right* **77**
Affording the move   77
Looking for the ideal property   79
Planning building work   80
Buying the property   82
Grants   85
Moving on   86

9 *Working from home*   **88**
Working from home successfully   88
Action plan 9.1   91
Where do we stand?   96

10 *Understanding your property*   *98*
   Getting in touch with the finer detail   98
   Doing your research   99
   Building up the contacts   104
   Getting in and keeping out   105
   Reaching a happy understanding   107

11 *Business plans, budgets and cash flow*   *108*
   Business plans   108
   Cash flow   112
   Simple book-keeping   114
   Money in the future   116

12 *Money makes the world go round*   *117*
   Money matters – it sure does!   118
   The bell curve concept   124

13 *Questions and answers: getting ready to go*   *127*
   Onwards and upwards   143

Appendix 1: Walking the talk   *145*
   Starting off   145
   The middle years   146
   Living abroad   148
   Home again   148
   Another sea change   151
   The answer   152
   Self-catering in the Highlands   154

Appendix 2: Useful reference sources   *155*
   Planning and setting up your business   155
   Running a business   156
   Training you and your staff   156
   Self-development   157

Finding small businesses in the country   157
Accounting software packages   157
Grants   158
Moving house   158

Index   *159*

Preface

There is an ever-increasing interest in the prospects of both down-shifting and relocation, demonstrated through the number of newspaper and magazine articles, television programmes and familiarization workshops. The pressures of work and the stresses and strains of city life have raised the question in many people's minds as to whether there is an alternative way of living.

As we set out in Appendix 1, we reached the initial point of decision many years ago and have downshifted progressively in a variety of ways, with some but not all changes involving relocation. Prior to this, while in more mainstream employment, we moved between Scotland and England on several occasions, with a two-year spell living and working in Europe, so we had a wide experience base to call on when researching for this book.

Downshifting and relocation are certainly not for everyone, but the wide variety of options means that, with your eyes wide open, there is likely to be some level which meets your needs if your heart is really set on change. We can confidently claim that the chapters which follow will help you decide, through both question and factual detail, the degree to which you should follow your heart – and how ready you are for that downshifting decision.

The book is divided into two sections. The first will take you through a range of searching situations and questions to help you decide whether you are ready for the move. Having reached your decision, the second section will elaborate on the practical detail necessary for that change in your life. If you are still undecided by the end of Section One, reading the detail in the second section might help you make up your mind.

We have tried to cover as wide a range as possible of both activities and locations in reviewing the options and priorities, but it goes without saying that when you are closer to a decision regarding your future, you should talk to those who are already involved in similar occupations. You should visit your short-listed locations (at various times of the year, if at all possible). In Appendix 2, you will find a list of useful websites which will offer you current information and detail beyond the level that we can ever hope to provide in a book. The internet is a valuable information source.

When making your decisions, do seek as much advice as possible, both professional and from people who have actually 'walked the talk'. Consider your options as objectively – but as widely – as possible. In the end, however, if you really want to do something – and your business plan figures stack up OK – take a bit of a gamble and go for it. Having taken the plunge, and still finding a range of opportunities opening up to us to broaden our downshifting experience, we would recommend it highly. Your attitude to life has to change and priorities and needs will vary and perhaps downsize, but the improved freedom, satisfaction and overall quality of life will make you wonder why you ever wavered at the point of decision.

Read the book, respond to the questions, think carefully, discuss widely – and good luck!

Chris and Gillean Sangster

Relocation and downshifting: introduction

Perhaps you have a little nagging voice in the back of your head somewhere, suggesting that you should be thinking of a major change of direction in your life. When you watch a programme on TV where people are considering a relocation or describing a complete change of life or work focus which they have achieved, perhaps you answer the voice with a quiet 'I could do that'. If you have these kinds of feelings periodically, consider the following:

- Have you ever stood face-to-back in an underground train on an August afternoon and wondered why you're doing it?
- Do you regularly find yourself crawling along in a queue of traffic for what seems like for ever – and are still miles from home?
- Have you sat viewing the piles of paperwork on your desk and wondered whether you'll ever see clear wood veneer again?
- Is it part of your key Sunday activity to look through the country property section of the newspapers and think, 'What would I give to live there'?
- Have you ever watched someone do as a job what you only touch on as a hobby and thought, 'I would rather be doing that'?

- Have you ever sat looking about you in your present house and thought, 'What am I doing here?'?
- Have you ever driven past a cottage in the country with a For Sale sign outside and fallen in love with it?

If you have, this book is for you.

What's the plan?

This book will look at some of the key implications of downshifting and relocation and consider the main criteria you can use to judge whether the time is right for you. We'll review the pros and cons of living in different parts of the country and provide ways for you to judge what level of country living is best for you. This could be roses round the porch door in the middle of a village, that isolated croft house surrounded by acres of your very own land, or myriad other options. Specific chapters will check out the finer points of selecting and purchasing a property and the realities of using part of your home for running your business, whether it be B & B, office for networking assignments or art and craft studio. We'll consider all the options.

Although we lived in Europe for a couple of years, we will focus on relocation within the UK, while acknowledging that many of the thought processes leading towards deciding to downshift will be similar, regardless of where you finally relocate. You may already be conscious through reading in the press that relocation abroad is a very country-specific exercise, with legal systems, property laws and local council or equivalent arrangements varying dramatically between countries and sometimes within different areas of the same country. If your sights are set abroad, we recommend that you consult books and reference sources which concentrate on each particular country, to avoid problems at a later stage of the exercise.

Work/life balance

With some thoughts towards your personal work/life balance, we'll review the options for changing your way of life – and how you can keep life and work as separate as you wish when working from a home base. Assuming that the relocation is more likely to be from town to country, we'll discuss the finer points of keeping your property up and running, considering possible obstacles such as:

- septic tanks
- private water supplies
- local tradesmen
- the possibility of living miles from the nearest large town.

Special attention will be focused on the finer points of running a business which allows you to earn enough to live on while still enjoying the relaxed country atmosphere you crave when you're stuck in that underground train or traffic jam.

So, let's get down to business. How do we define the difference between relocation and downshifting?

Downshifting and relocation

The dictionary defines *relocation* as 'movement to a new district of work or residence', with emphasis on the change of place or location from one point to another. *Downshifting* can be defined as being 'movement from a way of life and work to a lower, less stressful level'. You could, fairly evidently, relocate from, say, London to Newcastle while continuing to work in the same or a similar job for your current company. This might have little effect on your work/life balance, although it might give you a less stressful journey to and from work. By our definitions, it would involve relocation but not downshifting.

As an alternative but additional step along the relocation/downshifting path, you could for example be a solicitor who lives and works in London and who decides to move to the Bath area. There you might take up a position with a legal and estate agency practice, with perhaps your partner giving up full-time employment. This would involve an element of downshifting as well as relocation but not entail working from home (unless this was within your partner's game plan). The book will consider a range of such options, with the implications of each.

Getting more focused

The type of relocation which we're considering, therefore, will include at least some degree of downshifting in order for there to be any point in going through the process. As the old adage goes, moving house is one of the most stressful things you can do, bar divorce. Add the potential of changing your lifestyle, setting up to be self-employed, kissing goodbye to a regular income and probably even dragging teenage children away from their much-loved urban haunts and you have an amalgam that must beat divorce by a short straw.

Are we trying to put you off the whole exercise? We certainly are not! Are we trying to present the situation as objectively as possible to allow you to prepare yourself properly and thoroughly? We certainly are.

Value for money

In Britain, it's a key pastime to regularly check on the value of your current property and discuss what this sum would buy in other parts of the country. As a reality check, the days when the half a million from your two-bedroomed Kensington flat or whatever would buy a castled estate in Scotland are largely gone, unless the aforementioned castle needs twice that amount spent on it to make it weathertight and habitable.

There certainly are variable values around the country, however, and if you're realistic, your downshifting in terms of job and income can still result in having a more flexible, relaxed lifestyle than you currently enjoy, in a property with grounds and facilities that you can only dream about at present. The chapters which follow will take you through the process of making the judgements necessary to decide whether those dreams will be turned into realities.

Personal experience

As you will read in Appendix 1, we have moved between Scotland and England several times, have lived in rented accommodation in Brussels for a couple of years and have owned a variety of properties. These have ranged from our first home, a one-bedroomed terraced cottage in a Scottish village costing little over the equivalent of a year's salary in the 1970s, to a 500-year-old thatched and timber-framed manor house, which we sold for what can be smugly referred to as 'a tidy sum'. Like many others, much of our financial flexibility can be put down to the purchase of a relatively run-down London property with potential, which we sold 14 years later at a very healthy profit.

Moving from London to Wiltshire and from Wiltshire to the West Highlands of Scotland allowed us to get more for our money, certainly in pure property terms. The selection of location and facilities has allowed us also to revise our work/life balance in order to downshift to a more enjoyable, flexible lifestyle than possible when conventionally employed, while maintaining a reasonable income. In the world of checks and balances, what we may have lost in safe, regular salary earning, we have infinitely more than made up for in quality and enjoyment of life. That, in our judgement, is crucial. That is what this book will help you achieve, with eyes wide open.

Being realistic

Objective decision making is very important when going through the process of changing your whole way of life quite dramatically. Decisions regarding relocation and downshifting should not be engendered by an absolute hatred of your current job and/or location. If they are, you're liable to make subjective judgements which you will live to regret. If, for example, you've spent most of your adult life in the middle of a town but are growing weary of living cheek by jowl with neighbours you don't like, the immediate solution of a cottage in the middle of nowhere in the Scottish Highlands may not seem so wise in deepest winter if the power fails and the water pipes freeze. Or maybe you can take the challenge in your stride?

In order to check this out, we always strongly advise people who are thinking of moving to a new area to make a point of visiting – and staying in – the area at different times of the year. You can find that some places which veritably buzz with activity in the height of summer draw in their limbs like a hibernating tortoise for four or five months over the winter. Is that what you want? It may be, but then again ... You must make the judgement because it's you who will be living with your decision.

▦ Reality check

Don't think about selling up and downshifting from town to country on a whim to 'see how you get on' in some rural idyll for a few years. If you do, you can be fairly certain that, financially, you'll have eaten into the amount you made from selling the house in town – and probably can't afford to buy it back to pick up on your former lifestyle. If you're thinking about self-sufficiency in Wales, rent an allotment near home for a while first and experience the amount of effort involved in growing a row of carrots to half the size you buy in the supermarket! This book will help you make these types of decisions objectively – and save the heartache later.

Getting your sums right

Be realistic about the earning potential of your relocation and down-shifting plans, especially for the initial months. In writing business plans, it's very easy to fall into the trap of including year-on-year income increases which you know the bank manager loves to read, without having any real idea where that income's coming from – or the real level of investment or expenditure necessary to make these projected incomes possible. It's a natural reaction to start off house hunting with a particular budget, which then rises like a thermom-eter in a heatwave as you're tempted by what's available over the financial horizon. Remember that you have to pay the mortgage in the quiet months as well as the successful ones – don't create a mill-stone for your neck which will overwhelm any improved lifestyle you have set out to achieve.

At this point, you may be thinking there are a lot of 'don'ts' creeping into the text. Are they trying to put us off totally and if so, what's the point in us reading further? No, the 'don'ts' are there to get you in the right frame of mind to consider your options fully. Only by doing this will you appreciate the relocation process as a bigger picture which you will gradually tailor to suit your particular priorities.

Objective thinking

Planning objectively, you'll be in a better position to decide what you really want to do and where you really want to go. You'll be able to better judge locations and price brackets which will then allow you to do what you want to do in a sustainable way. We, for example, have set up a holiday cottage business. We worked out that the minimum number of letting properties which would bring us an acceptable income over the year would be three. Knowing the sum of money which selling the property we owned at the time would realise, we could then assess the highest amount we could spend on purchasing these three letting units and a home for ourselves.

This figure had implications on the choice of areas around Britain where suitable properties were within our price range. (We had already decided to stay in this country – buying abroad would of course have been another option.) Where we underestimated in our calculations was in judging the overall cost of refurbishing and structurally altering the property we purchased in order to produce these four living spaces. This was further complicated by the difficulty of judging the amount of work involved in converting an older building, where you seldom know the extent of the job until you start removing the surface coatings.

So, however well you plan, there are always pitfalls and traps along the way. Invariably, once you've got your first bank loan, additional loans are more easily forthcoming. However, tread that path with care. It may seem like the answer to the problem to extend your borrowing – but just remember the cloud of the monthly repayment. As a benchmark, you can ask yourself the question, 'Are my repayments in January and February going to colour my enjoyment of the Christmas festivities?' And if the answer is 'no', is it because you can cope or is it because you've gone past caring? Think objectively – it may be boring but it helps to support your chosen work/life balance, long term.

▦ The range of our investigations

A rapid scan through the contents pages will give you a taste of what's to come. This book is mainly concerned with the property side of relocation and downshifting. The specifics of downshifting and the choices and decisions open to you may be discussed separately. It will, however, be necessary to consider the implications of downshifting from time to time, where decisions associated with your plans will have a knock-on effect on relocation choices. So, the book will review locations, building types, facilities and the variety of requirements on offer to help you achieve the kind of work/life balance you prefer.

We'll consider the various options for working from home and what requirements this places on the design of the property itself, reviewing some of the priorities for setting up a professional office within your home. We'll share our experiences – and those of others – regarding the upkeep and maintenance of larger and rural properties and compare and contrast our dealings with tradespeople around the country, in both urban and rural settings. Periodically, we'll include questionnaires and other forms of interactive checklists to give you the opportunity to review your priorities and decisions as you gradually refine your personal master plan towards designing your new life and location.

So, what are we waiting for? Let's get down to it!

Part One

Deciding whether downshifting and relocation is right for you

Are you ready?

A major part of the success in deciding to downshift/relocate is tied up with the kind of person you are. You'll meet problems and challenges in your new life. There's no getting away from the fact that personality has a great deal to do with the way you'll react to them. What are your priorities for your new life? Do you know what you want in terms of location and future employment (or ways of making enough to live on)? How close do you want to be to friends, facilities, entertainment or towns? What exactly are your options? This is what we are now ready to consider in detail.

Why do you want to downshift?

The reasons for your decision are important. But just as importantly, you should be considering whether they are valid reasons.

Some of your reasons might be negative.

- *Tired of your present job.* Not really a sufficient reason in itself. What is it about the present job that bores you? The people? The office or work environment? The actual work? You could consider moving to a new job without moving house.

- *Working long hours.* Again not a sufficient reason in itself. Can you cut down on the hours or should you just be looking for a different job?
- *Fed up with the commuting.* This is a difficult one. So many people have to live at a distance from their place of work. Your move to the country may mean that initially anyway you are still commuting – perhaps from a greater distance but less often. You might consider working from home part of the week or commuting to a smaller town/city involving an easier journey.
- *Jaded with city life.* Are you sure of this? Have you perhaps just had a run of difficult weeks? Or is this a more long-term feeling? City life can be both tiring and stimulating – be sure that in your move out of the city you won't miss the buzz.
- *Getting more for your money property wise.* This is very tempting but is not the best of reasons on its own. Studying the estate agents' leaflets or reading *Country Life* provides a few hours of speculation and fun but is definitely not in itself a solid basis for a future life.

And some of your reasons might be positive.

- *Want to bring up children in a healthier environment.* Consider though whether the children want to move. This may not concern you, but it should. It is not a problem if they are still fairly young, but once they reach an age where they have established friendships and schools it becomes more difficult. True, many children can make new friends easily, but you will have to sell them the benefits of the move – perhaps a larger bedroom, a school with better outdoor activities, access to new hobbies such as white water rafting, sailing, canoeing, climbing, riding, etc.
- *Want to establish 'real' values for living.* This can be a tricky one. Those 'real' values are very personal ones. Do you mean getting away from staring at a computer screen, visiting clubs, pubs and cinemas and being led by the craze of the moment? This is possible, but in this age of easy communication, much of this will follow you wherever you go. The opportunities are there, but you'll have to reach out and take them. People in the country certainly have more time to spend chatting to you and to each

other. Shopping can take longer for all the right reasons. You'll learn more about your neighbours and they will learn about you. Everything is on a more personal level, but you may find this difficult to adjust to if you're used to a more anonymous way of life. However, when you're in difficulties or need help with a practical problem, you'll hopefully find that in general people are more willing to help. If by 'real' you mean close to nature in all its moods, then this is certainly true. We have a private water supply and in the warm, dry weather popular with the guests in our cottages, the rivers run very low. The rain is a welcome relief. Glorious sunsets, amazing views of the mountains with the first snows of winter, and the red and gold leaves of the beech trees down at the lochside in the autumn are all sights we never tire of.

- *Want a more flexible lifestyle.* Your lifestyle will certainly change and this is perhaps one of the best things about the downshifting ideal. Flexibility in work patterns, in ideas and in day-to-day living can make a real difference. You'll be taking more responsibility for your life and will not be so dependent on the decisions of others.

- *Have a love of the countryside.* Do you spend weekends in the country? Are your holidays invariably in the countryside? Do you dream of looking out of your window at fields and trees? Or at the sea? Have you visited the country in the winter months? In the rain? Do you know about public transport in the area of your choice? Will the school run be a considerably longer one than it is at the moment?

- *Want to spend more time with each other and the family.* Yes, you can certainly achieve this by downshifting. But then we consider this a vital and enjoyable part of the change. As my friend used to say about life, 'this is not a dress rehearsal'. Children are only young once and this will give you the opportunity to spend time with them at all the important stages of their growing up. It will also give you the chance to spend more time with each other, making decisions that are important to you both and perhaps taking up new interests or working together to establish yourselves in your new environment.

Action plan 2.1

Some of these reasons are more important than others. It is up to you to judge for yourself. You should be aware of both the positive and negative aspects above which may be real issues for you. Check them through and write the totals of those which you consider to be significant below.

Number of positive	Number of negative

Make a note of any other positive reasons you have for relocating. Are there any more reasons you have for the move that you might consider to be negative? On balance, then, are there more positive than negative reasons? Or is it the other way round?

Assuming that you are still thinking positively about your decision to relocate, let's now look at the sort of personality you have. Are you suited for this adventure?

■ What kind of person are you?

Are you the kind of person who can make a success of this new life you are planning? These are some of the questions you should perhaps ask yourself:

- *Do you make new friends easily?* You may well be moving away from all your friends and relatives. Although you will almost certainly be welcoming your old friends at weekends and holidays, you'll be very lonely if you find it hard to make new friends.

  Yes   No

- *Are you generally optimistic?* Much can go wrong on a day-to-day basis when you are building your new life – it helps to see things positively and not to get easily depressed.

  Yes   No

- *Are you unconcerned with career paths?* You will possibly be leaving careers behind. Does this bother you or are you happy to lead a less structured life? When your old friends come to visit you and discuss their high salaries and exotic holidays, will this bother you?

   Yes   No

- *Do you have an open mind?* Basically, are you ready for anything that is thrown at you? Can you consider new options and change tack if necessary?

   Yes   No

- *Are you realistic?* Can you see clearly that there will be problems as well as advantages with your new way of living? And can you deal honestly with those problems?

   Yes   No

- *Are you prepared to work hard towards your goal?* It may well take a lot more effort than anticipated to establish yourself in your new life. Your success will largely depend on your efforts and determination to see things through. Initially you may be working longer hours than before and there might be periods of sustained effort which are exhausting. Here I am reminded of the setting up of our cottages when the builder took longer than anticipated to finish a cottage and, with a fixed booking already made for a certain date, we had only ten days to paint, wallpaper and furnish the cottage.

   Yes   No

- *Do you welcome challenges?* Your new life may throw up problems that you hadn't thought of. Can you deal with new ideas and work towards solutions to unexpected problems?

   Yes   No

- *Can you cope with relative isolation?* It may be that you'll choose a new home at a distance from any town or village. Can you cope with not seeing another human being (except your family) for days? This will have an impact on where you choose to live and is an important consideration.

  Yes   No

- *Can you exist on a low income, at least for a while?* You'll need savings to see you over the gap between leaving your old life and establishing your new one. Don't underestimate the necessity for this. You may well have to live at a level below that to which you are accustomed. Are you prepared for this? Can you deal with the fact that you can no longer buy special cheeses or an expensive bottle of wine? Or go out for meals?

  Yes   No

- *Are you prepared to get your hands dirty?* We mean this literally. Are you ready to unblock a drain? To paint and wallpaper? To dig a drainage ditch in the pouring rain? To grow vegetables (if this is what you decide)? To deal with a broken fence? In fact, are you a practical person?

  Yes   No

- *Can you turn your hand to new skills?* Are you adaptable? Tradesmen are expensive and may take some time to come. You can save time and money by doing many of those odd jobs yourself. You can prepare for this by taking evening classes or reading manuals.

  Yes   No

- *Can you cope with the insecurity of an irregular salary?* The disadvantages of working at that office job with long hours are balanced by the advantage of a regular income. Can you deal with money appearing at irregular intervals?

  Yes   No

● *Are you unconcerned with appearances?* If you are building up a business, most of your money will go towards that. After all, it's the business which will hopefully support you in the future. You won't be able to spend money for a while on your house, car, clothes or a holiday. Will it concern you to welcome your visitors to a less than perfect environment? Can you cope with neighbours or friends discussing their holidays? Would you mind if you had to keep the old car for a year or two longer? And do you mind not buying any new clothes except essentials? (It is worth bearing in mind here that you probably won't need so many new clothes living in the country.)

Yes   No

Action plan 2.2

How many 'yes' answers and how many 'no' answers do you have?

Number of 'yes' answers	Number of 'no' answers

You may have answered 'yes' to most of these questions but 'no' to only some of them. Can you see a way round the problems you may have identified in making your 'no' responses? Think about each for a moment or two.

If, on the other hand, you have a large number of 'no' responses, perhaps you should be reconsidering your position fairly seriously at this point.

So, we've looked at your reasons for moving to a new life and discussed whether you are the sort of person who can make a success of it. Now let's look at the future.

Assuming now that you are ready to downshift and have the right sort of personality to succeed, exactly what are your priorities for your new life? What practical considerations are there? How do you intend to live your new life or set up your business?

Changing direction

First of all, how will you live? Will you:

- continue in your present job but to a lesser extent, perhaps working from home some days
- continue the same sort of employment but in a smaller town
- leave your career path and try something new
- combine two options, with one of you maintaining that regular salary and the other taking the opportunity to break into something new?

Looking at the options

If you decide to try something new, are you considering extending a hobby you already have or making a complete break with the past? Some of the choices you might be considering are:

- opening a bed and breakfast
- self-catering
- pottery/painting/sculpture, etc
- running a shop or gallery
- writing for profit
- farming, market gardening, plant nursery
- fishing
- a pony trekking or horse riding business
- opening a restaurant
- running a pub or hotel
- a specialist service, possibly in such areas as website design, garden landscaping, etc.
- a trade – plumber, electrician, painter and decorator, etc.

Getting down to detail

Your list of priorities will depend on your choice. To run a restaurant successfully you will need customers. Some of the restaurants in the tourist areas of Britain, for example, close down during the winter as there is not a sufficient local population to support them. A hotel may be a seasonal option too, particularly in the remote Highlands or by the sea, unless you pick your location carefully. Can you get supplies easily? If you are keen on organic produce, is it available there?

Running a shop or a gallery may well require a town setting. Are you considering the right size of town with likely potential customers?

If you're set on farming or market gardening, you must decide on the type. Are you interested in arable, dairy or sheep farming, for example? The countryside of Britain is full of variety and the type of farming you plan will of course affect your choice of location.

If you're considering running a bed and breakfast or holiday cottages, you will not want to be in an area where there are large numbers of similar establishments and yet you need to be where the visitors will come. There is usually a range of existing businesses on the market, but what in your business plan makes you convinced that you can have better long-term success than the present owners? Will you want an area where there are already well-known tourist attractions – castles, beautiful scenery, stately homes, distilleries, national parks? If you are planning an all-year-round business, would you think about being close to climbing or skiing territory?

Clarifying your priorities

Once you're clearer in your mind about the type of business you may be running, you will be able to focus on possible locations and the priorities that are high on your list. Consider the following questions.

- Will you still need good links to London?
- Do you need to be in or near a town?
- Is living in a tourist area essential?
- Is it important to be close to good schools? Will a local village school suffice or do you need a secondary school within reach?
- Will you need efficient local public transport? Country areas are notorious for poor transport links. Tied in with this might be the need for two cars. Will you be able to afford to run them?

- What will you need in the way of land? You might be considering farming or keeping horses.
- Do you still want to have access to cinemas, theatres, concerts and restaurants?
- Do you want to live in really remote country? Or close to a village?
- Must you be within easy reach of friends or relations? How easy? We are at the opposite end of the country from our daughter who lives on the south coast but we can fly from a local airport in the Scottish Highlands to Gatwick in a remarkably short time.
- Would you like to live by the sea? Or a large lake? Or on a riverbank?
- Do you want close neighbours or would you prefer to live at a distance from other houses?
- What will you require in the way of property for your new life and business? Do you need a workshop, studio or extra space in your house for a study?
- One of your main priorities should be the happiness of both or all of you. Is there enough for both of you to be happy and occupied in your new location? If one of you is dissatisfied, the project will not be a success.

Action Plan (2.3)

List six of your main priorities and try to put them in order of importance to you.

1
2
3
4
5
6

▓ **Moving forward**

We've taken a look at the reasons why you want to downshift/relocate and whether they are positive or negative. Only you can decide at this stage – and later on – whether there are enough positive reasons for you to make the move. Beware, though, if you're thinking of going ahead without being convinced on the positive front.

We've also considered whether you are the sort of person who will succeed in this new life. What about your partner? Do you form a good team for the venture? Do your personalities complement each other?

Now it's time to start thinking positively about the future. Your answers to Action plan 2.3 will help you to plan your way forward. Let's take the next step!

Deciding what's best for you

Although we are focusing mainly on the thoughts involved in relocation, it's logical to consider first some of the key activity options open to you. These will cover aspects such as your career, personal development and the opportunities available for downshifting. This is a very personal thing – we're not in the game of trying to force you down any particular routes. This is the age of empowerment – it's you who will make the decisions because it's mainly you who will live with them, fine-tuning the ideas as necessary to get the best fit for your particular needs. Your initial thoughts and decisions are thus very important.

Do bear in mind the possibility that your decisions are quite likely to affect others – partner, children, spouse and so on: it's their life as well as yours. Remember also that, however well you plan, some things won't work out as you thought they would, and some situations will undoubtedly change from the way they were when you did your initial planning.

So, if you're thinking of future plans as a twosome or a family, make sure you include the full picture in the frame. If your dream is to run a sheep farm halfway up a Scottish hillside, check that your partner is happy about all the implications. Initially, this involves establishing in some detail what these implications would be. Talk to those who know. Best of all, if you can, talk to someone who is actually doing it. Keep an objective mind open to the strengths and weaknesses of your cunning plan. It may realize your needs, but equally it might have so many blocks and concerns that an objective review will show that it's really, honestly, a non-starter.

Carrying out a SWOT analysis

This is a business idea, which is very useful in life generally. Using it helps you remain as objective as possible and it also encourages you to compare like with like if you're trying to come up with a preferred strategy. For our purposes, we can take the letters to represent:

S   Strengths
W   Weaknesses
O   Opportunities
T   Timescales/Threats (as appropriate)

So, taking our Scottish Highland shepherd idea as a mini case study, let's run through the considerations for James, a teacher who is married and currently resident in Putney, south London.

Can teacher become shepherd?

Strengths
- Would give me the open-air life I crave.
- Living would be cheaper than my present city life.
- Overall would provide me with more free time to pursue interests.
- Profits from present flat sale would reduce any future mortgage.
- Young child (aged 4) would gain benefits from rural life.

Weaknesses
- Wife does not have driving licence and has lived an urban life to date.
- I have limited knowledge about sheep husbandry.
- Doubts about annual profitability, without additional income.

- Not sure, as a family, how we would fit into rural village life.
- Lack of awareness about local schooling arrangements.

Opportunities
- Dramatic change of way of life and work/life balance.
- Possibilities for self and wife to develop artistic interests.
- Potential for income from marketing art commercially.
- Healthier lifestyle.
- Involvement in working with livestock.

Threats
- Probability of being able to gain enough income, year on year.
- Acceptance and enjoyment of rural living by all parties involved.
- Lack of knowledge about animal husbandry and crofting.
- Availability of funds for adequate land to make project viable.
- Ability to cope with possible extremes of weather.

So, with these considerations in mind, how would you advise our good friend James? Are there more pluses than minuses? Does he have some preparatory homework to do before proceeding much further down the line? I think he has.

Action plan 3.1

Think of at least four areas which James needs to check out or discuss. For a start, James needs to:

1
2
3
4

Check your ideas against the suggested answers at the end of this chapter.

Keeping an open mind

Let's keep positive, though. We're not saying that James should forget his pipe dreams and settle down to a life of broadening the upper fourth's knowledge of French participles. What we are saying is that, when you're going through this initial reality check process, you have to respond openly to the issues that it raises.

- Are your personal desires blinding you to the valid concerns displayed by your partner or family?
- Do you need to find out more about the activities and way of life that you fancy, to make sure that the reality will be more or less as attractive as the dream?
- Do you need some experience of living in the potential geographic area(s)?
- Would you really, happily, settle into the lifestyle which your plans can finance?
- Could you complete a business plan or at least put some figures to your plans?

There are many other considerations but these are probably enough to be thinking about at this early stage.

The options open to you

This possible range of options open to you really is as broad as your imagination, lateral thought and current or future skills and knowledge capabilities – referred to as 'competency levels' in the trade nowadays. Without getting too complicated, however, there are considerations which will help you check the likelihood that your dreams will reach some level of reality.

Let's say, for example, that you're artistic. Pottery, painting, glass blowing, basket making ... you name it, you'll find them all represented in rural communities. There is, however, a difference between producing artistic pieces of some description and making a living by being an artist. What are some of the initial considerations?

- Check outlets: could you sell your products through local galleries or shops?
- What is it that sells in the area and will your artistic standards allow you to feel happy producing this (i.e. are plaster Nessies or cartoons of beefeaters your thing)?
- As an extension of this thinking, could you perhaps practise 'split creativity', producing 'bread and butter' products to support your other, greater creativity?
- Would you like to have a working studio/gallery to sell your products? If so, this may have implications on finding a property with a more public location.
- Would you prefer to work solo or would there be a commercial logic in joining up with some other artists, sharing a studio or gallery outlet?
- How seasonal would the market be, and if you have a 5–8-month season, how do you go about paying the rent or mortgage for the rest of the year?

In the same way that a lack of interest in the paperwork and organisational side of business has been the downfall of many a self-employed tradesman (although the public is calling out for their services), a lack of commercial awareness is the downfall of many an artist trying to make a living from their art. There is limited point in lining your studio walls with ever-increasing stacks of unsold canvases – it's moving them onto the sitting room walls of your visiting clientele that keeps food on the table and a roof overhead. With a bit of thought and effort, however, you can find the formula for producing 'must-have, marketable product', as the saying goes.

▓ Being objective

All you need to do is keep an eye on the bigger picture – and be honest and truthful to yourself. Discussing your plans with others – and we mean really discussing openly – will put you in the position of having to justify your decisions and priorities. If you're objective enough, you'll begin to see where you haven't thought your plan through clearly. I know, in my heart, that when I'm having difficulty in trying to explain an idea to my partner, and am beginning to get annoyed because 'she just won't understand and is being obtuse', the problem really lies in my not having thought through the situation properly. So, either I go away and do just that, or the two of us talk through the problem and usually reach an agreed outcome. It must be said, however, that we are blessed with a relationship which can handle that level of objectivity, which is a real benefit.

Having a 'Blue Water'

This is the phrase we use for our impromptu business decision meetings. I used to work with a company with a very fancy boardroom, with posh blue bottles of Welsh water on its massive table. The company's great and good (as well as some less great and less good) gathered periodically for long, heated and sometimes openly devious discussions about policy. I can still picture the blue bottles, though many of the corporate faces have faded into dim memories.

Our 'Blue Waters' happen when the need and mood arise – in the bathroom, at breakfast, in the office, while out walking the dogs, even sometimes sitting down at the dining table, so that relevant papers and documents can be consulted properly. When the time and atmosphere are right, reality checks of the latest idea can usually progress quite rapidly. Revision, postponement, sometimes rejection follow, but overall the result is progress in our bigger picture.

This type of objective thinking should not be seen as a threat to your dreams; rather, it should highlight any area which needs further review and perhaps a few amendments. Going through the process can sometimes be painful, where you find yourself trying to defend your dream against what you see at times as cynical questioning (or worse). But work through it if you can. Not only will it show up some of the planning defects which require further consideration, it will also sharpen your ideas and lines of argument, preparing you for the moment when you really have to sell your case, to bank managers, local government wonks or potential customers.

■ Case study

An urban-based friend of ours desperately wanted to set up a workshop to construct furniture. He had the skills and the marketing contacts and had identified a property out on a Scottish moor, which had a large barn workshop, a home and an additional letting property.

So far, so good: alternative means of income, with the potential for income streams throughout the year. The property was, however, about 12 miles from the nearest village and small shop and was exposed to severe winter weather. In addition, it did not have mains electricity, relying on power from a diesel generator. Our friend's wife doesn't drive and a resident adult member of the family cannot drive for medical reasons. This friend would have to be away from home for extended periods of time, installing the furniture. The family's existence to date had always been in a large, industrialized town.

Run a SWOT check on that scenario and I think you'd agree that the outcome would be along the lines of downshifting opportunity – good; location – pretty bad.

This, as indicated already, is where your plans for downshifting have a strong influence on your selection of location. In the example above, we have an indication of how downshifting plans must involve the whole family situation rather than merely a change of occupation.

So much for considering the plans of others. How about yourself?

Action plan 3.2

Here's a list of questions to consider. Jot down your responses to each of these on a piece of paper. Better still, use a notebook so that you can store your responses for later reference.

1. Which parts of any present employment do you enjoy?
2. Do you enjoy networking with others?

3. How well do you think you can sell yourself and your products/ skills to others?

4. Do you have any hobbies/interests which are/could be commercially productive?

5. Are you thinking of the type of existence (e.g. hotel) which requires a 24/7 life?

6. Why are you considering changing your way of life?

7. How good are you (singly or collectively) at managing money in your household?

8. In your area of expertise, what do you think people want to pay money to have?

9. To what extent are you aware of the processes involved in gaining work/contracts?

10. List your main marketable skills, then rank them in order of competence.

There are no right and wrong answers to these questions. You should, however, have found it possible to respond in some detail to each of the questions. After completing the questionnaire, you may also feel more confident about possible ways forward to meet your personal downshifting plans

Choosing your skills

Let's clarify one thing at this point. It *is* possible to downshift without making a major change in your occupation.

- Earlier, we described a London lawyer moving to a more laid-back area like Bath and becoming a solicitor/estate agent. A change of focus and a reduction in stress levels undoubtedly.
- Equally, a mathematics teacher in a Glasgow comprehensive could move to become a headteacher of a two-teacher primary school in the Western Isles. Some changes necessary here but likely to be a lot more relaxed.
- You could go from a full-time job to doing the same or a very similar job part-time, in order to give yourself time to develop a

parallel interest. This could be achieved without moving company or location, or could incorporate a move to cheaper accommodation to reduce regular outgoings.

You can doubtless think of other similar situations. The overall point here is that downshifting doesn't have to come about through hatred and dread of your present occupation. You may just want to shift the emphasis of levels of responsibility, stress, involvement and so on, to potentially open the door to combining elements of your existing job with additional activities. Short of this, you could see the act of downshifting as an opportunity to reassess your personal work/life balance.

Action plan 3.3

Here are a few additional questions to ask yourself.

- What level of change would you be happy to make for your preferred situation?
- What elements of any present job would you like to continue doing?
- What additional activities and skills areas would you like to include?
- Where would you ideally like to live to carry out this new lifestyle?
- Combining these thoughts, is an overall strategy becoming apparent?

You should be beginning to focus to some extent on what your preferences might be.

▓ Review time

So, where do we stand at present?

- We've considered a way of objectively reviewing possible ideas.
- We've established the need to think through the effects on all parties involved.
- We've identified some of the background research which we have to carry out.
- We've gone through the process of considering the range of options open to us.
- We've run through a few examples to show the need for reality checks.
- We've reviewed some of our personal skills, priorities and opportunities.

So, quite a few considerations so far – and many more to come as we gradually focus more closely on what you're good at, what you want to do, how you can see a viable living coming from the activities, and what you have identified as a package of ideas and opportunities which satisfy all parties involved as much as possible.

▓ When 'what' becomes 'where'

As we have already established, many of your activity or downshifting options will have direct implications on where you consider setting up and the type of property you will need. Some downshifting opportunities can be carried out from virtually anywhere. If you have established outlets for your skills, as a writer, specialist consultant or service technician, for example, any travelling involved will be on an ad-hoc basis and can be more easily accommodated. There's a wide range of opportunities out there.

So, now that we've mentally opened a battery of doors to welcome in a whole range of possible downshifting opportunities, and seen the areas where location becomes relevant, it's time to focus more specifically on this.

Check point: Action plan 3.1

So, how did you manage these responses? It's really a case of considering the weaknesses and threats, and delving more deeply. This will give James considerations such as:

- go on a course on animal husbandry to see whether it really suits;
- check on the realities of rural living by spending time there – at different times of the year;
- work out an informed and detailed business plan, to convince yourself, not the bank manager;
- discuss projected profit and loss accounts with both a farmer and an accountant;
- research the availability of suitable properties with adequate land (quantity and quality);
- discuss the detail of farm support subsidies etc. to understand how the grant system works;
- discuss the need for wife to pass driving test if living in remote area;
- once you have narrowed down possible locations, visit schools and check facilities.

You may have others, but they will follow the same line of thinking. This will help you approach the possibility of downshifting with your eyes open, even if some of the answers prove to be slightly unsettling or disappointing. Better to face the realities now than when you're in the midst of lambing in the pouring rain!

Choosing your location

By now you'll probably have a good idea of what you want to do. You may well know the sort of area you want to live in but haven't made that final decision yet as to exactly where. It's important to look at all the options open to you as it is going to be vital to your future happiness and the success of your business. This chapter will present some of the possibilities for your consideration. We strongly recommend that you visit the specific areas you shortlist to get a real feel for the locations.

Britain has an incredibly varied countryside, ranging from wild mountains to idyllic villages among green fields to long open sea coasts and wide marshlands. The weather too will make an impact on where you want to be. Cornwall, Wales and the west coast of Scotland have high rainfall but a milder climate than the drier and colder east. In general, though, the further north you go, the colder it will be.

▣ Commuting territory

This need not be as restrictive as it sounds. When you think of commuting you may automatically think of London, but all over Britain people are travelling into cities to work. According to a study by the

RAC in 2003, Britons spend more time commuting than any other nation in Europe. The average British worker spends 22–25 minutes travelling each way to and from work, twice that of the Italians. In fact, commuting time varies in Britain from 19 minutes each way for the average worker in Wales to 56 minutes for the Central London worker. If your future life involves one of you carrying on with their present job, at least for a while, then this is something you'll have to consider.

Moving out of London to the countryside within commuting reach might be your favoured option. Check on the possibilities. We lived in Wiltshire for a number of years, when I worked first in London and then in Reading. Conveniently, many of the regular trains from Penzance to Paddington stopped at the small station in our nearby village of Pewsey. When we first moved there, it was not a well-known station and there were only about ten people waiting on the platform in the early morning. By the time we were thinking of moving on, the number had risen to over 50.

With the increasing popularity of the counties within reach of London however, house prices have risen steeply. Commuters are travelling longer and longer distances. One or two fellow travellers on that train were commuting daily from Devon. London is a special case, but it is worth considering breaking the link with the south-east of England and working in a different city. In the RAC study, the average commuting time for the north-east of England was shown to be a reasonable 21 minutes each way.

In Scotland, Edinburgh is expanding rapidly, pushing up house prices in all the surrounding villages. Commuters are now starting to look further afield, even as far as the Borders, although there is as yet no direct rail link. Newspaper articles laud Moffat, which is only a mile from the M74 and about 50 miles from Glasgow or Edinburgh, as a town with many attractions where commuters are buying homes. Dunfermline, the ancient capital of Scotland, is only four miles from the Forth Bridge and convenient for travelling to Edinburgh, Glasgow or Perth. Here and in many similar small towns, quality of life is a plus factor. Property is much cheaper and the family can benefit from a more peaceful existence and space to breathe.

If you don't have to commute, you have a far wider choice. Your business may of course dictate the sort of area you'll settle in. The following is not a comprehensive list, only a guide to your decision, but it may give you some new ideas, or simply confirm what you already know.

Coastal areas

Which do you prefer: wide, flat, sandy beaches or rocks and cliffs? Crowds or quiet? A few places you might consider are:

- the busy towns and villages of the south coast of England;
- the beautiful bays and cliffs of Cornwall and Devon;
- the wilder reaches of the Gower peninsula in Wales;
- the wide stretches of the north-east beaches of England;
- the picturesque coast of Fife;
- the glorious west of Scotland.

Life on the coasts of Britain is as varied as you make it. If you want to run a bed and breakfast, for example, you're looking for somewhere visitors will want to come to. But it must be right for you too. Devon and Cornwall are popular, but perhaps there are enough B & Bs there already. If you want cliffs and rocky shores, think of the coast of west Wales, of Dorset, of the north-east of England or the east and far north of Scotland. Perhaps you'd be happier in a resort such as Scarborough, Torquay, Aberystwyth, Ayr or Lyme Regis. If you want a more remote option, how about living in a lighthouse or an old coastguard's cottage?

The coast of the West Highlands is beautiful, with such places as Lochinver, Mallaig and Ullapool. Fishing villages have a great attraction and are sources of interest all year round. The coasts of Cornwall and the east of Scotland are full of them. Beachcombing, cliff path walking, swimming or just watching the changing face of the sea are enjoyable activities all year round (except the swimming perhaps!). Cold winds off the North Sea in winter and the damp sea haar creeping in over the land are features of some parts of the east coast. The west is wetter but the sea keeps frosts to a minimum and generally the weather is milder in winter.

Farm and arable land

During the foot and mouth outbreak in 2001 it became clear how much of Britain is involved in farming. If you mean to buy and run a farm, your area will be determined by the sort of farm you are looking for – arable, dairy or sheep, for example. However, you might be considering market gardening, a plant nursery or self-sufficiency. Check the local markets where you will see farmers and market gardeners with their produce. Many counties are ideal for this:

- Devon
- Hereford
- Norfolk
- Perthshire
- Angus
- Dumfries and Galloway
- Wiltshire.

If you want to run a farm, you need to know a great deal before you start. Unless you have lived or worked on a farm already, I would say it's potentially a rash choice. Theoretical knowledge is not enough for so practical a lifestyle, where a wrong decision can cause serious problems. If you are a small farmer, it is a precarious way to make a living unless you specialize.

Organic farming is increasingly popular these days. Take advice from those who are in the business already. Market gardening, too, can be an attractive option. The farmers' markets in towns and villages throughout Britain are growing in popularity as people become more concerned with what they are eating. Complete self-sufficiency is rare, but there is no reason why you should not make a success of growing most of your own vegetables. You could even consider selling to local greengrocers or setting up a shop on your property to sell extra produce.

Small towns and cities

Do you know the sort of town you are aiming for? Check the high streets and the local businesses. Are the streets busy with tourists? Is there a market for your business? Is there a good range of shops?

Some different categories to consider are:

- cathedral cities – Canterbury, Wells, York, Lincoln, etc.
- university towns – Cambridge, Durham, Exeter, Stirling, etc.
- market towns – Salisbury, Tavistock, Market Drayton, etc.
- historic towns – Chester, York, Rye, Bath, Edinburgh, etc.

Even with these four categories there is considerable overlap. There are so many more choices you can make.

Living in a small town or city can be a happy choice. You may have left the big city behind but you should still be able to have a high quality of life, with a good choice of schools, plenty of history, theatre and cinemas and a range of leisure activities. If you are used to city life, it isn't such a shock to the system to still be surrounded by cafes, bars, shops and restaurants, albeit on a smaller scale than before. You will also have the opportunity of getting out of the city much more easily to take advantage of the surrounding countryside. There are often semi-rural housing developments in new villages on the outskirts of cities which will let you enjoy the countryside, yet have all the amenities of town living. Some towns are surrounded by new housing developments though. Do you want to be part of this or do you prefer the more traditional housing in the centre?

If you opt for a market town, you have the daily or weekly activity of the market stalls and the possibility of a bargain. Is the town on the tourist trail though? Is it packed with visitors in the summer, making it impossible to park anywhere? Will these same visitors be good for your business or have you moved to get away from crowds?

Villages

There are many different types of rural living. For any particular individual, some will be more attractive – and viable – than others. This can create the need for compromise decisions if you are considering relocation with a partner. Where would your personal choice focus? Would it be on:

- the lovely villages of the Cotswolds;
- picture postcard villages in Sussex;
- old fishing villages in Devon, Cornwall, Fife;
- stone-built villages in the Lake District and the North Yorkshire moors;
- downland villages in Wiltshire?

Village life is very different from living in the town or city. Some villages, notably those within commuting distance of cities such as Bristol or London, are full of 'incomers'. Here it may be easy to settle in as most of the people living there have not been born and bred in the village. There are, however, still many small villages where families have lived for generations. Tractors drive through the streets leaving mud in their wake and cocks crow at inconvenient hours. Everybody knows everybody else. In many areas this is what a village is all about and it will be up to you to fit in and not rock the boat. After all, you chose to settle there.

Life in a small community can be tremendously rewarding and it is worth making the effort to be part of it. Village events, though probably less sophisticated than you may be used to, can be great fun. 'Go with the flow' as they say and enjoy them. Get involved!

If you have children, you need to know about the schools locally. Is there a village school or are the children bussed to the nearest town? What happens at secondary school level? What about activities for the children such as swimming pools, clubs and societies? Are there enough activities for you too? Will you miss your weekly visit to the gym or leisure centre?

Choose your village carefully. Some are relatively close to towns with all the amenities available while others are fairly remote with poor transport links. Shopping can be a problem. Is there a village store or newsagent? How far is it to a supermarket? Where is the nearest garage? What about a restaurant for that special evening out? Can you do without a delicatessen or wine bar? Is there a hotel or pub?

There are literally thousands of villages in Britain, most of which you have never seen. Visit as many as you can in the area you're considering.

Mountains and moorland

Once again, there is a wide and varied range. These might include:

- the Highlands of Scotland
- the Welsh mountains
- the Pennines
- the Dales
- the North Yorkshire Moors
- the Lake District.

Some of these areas, such as the Highlands, are more remote than others. This is something you may want to consider.

If the mountains and moors are your choice, then you really are going for the remote life. Two of your biggest problems will be transport and weather. The roads, though usually quieter than in other areas, are often slower. Distance tends to be measured not in miles but in time. For instance, the journey to Inverness, our closest city, takes one hour in winter and one and a quarter hours minimum in summer. This has nothing to do with the weather but everything to do with the tourists! The coach loads of summer visitors that tour Loch Ness cause delays for the rest of the traffic.

Our nearest sizeable supermarket is 30 miles away, although there are several smaller shops within a few miles. The best way is to think laterally. Plan your journeys to any town to include everything you need to do and work your way through the list. Food shopping, hair, hospital or dental appointments, buying birthday presents or cards (keep a stock of these), picking up paint or wallpaper or any other DIY goods and a visit to the cinema can all be slotted in.

On the plus side you will have magnificent scenery and a peaceful environment. The air is clear and there is no traffic to speak of once you are off the main road. The walks are wonderful. You do need to adapt to it, however. We occasionally have visitors enthusiastic for the country life who, after a few days, realize that this is not for them. There is no street lighting here and it's very dark at night. It's essential to check out the area first. If you live in a city you may not realize the degree of remoteness in some of these regions. What seems fantastic in the summer may not be so fantastic when the snow comes or, worse I think, after several days of driving rain.

Islands

If island living is for you, consider not only the more obvious such as the

- Isle of Wight
- Isle of Man
- Channel Islands (need to be very well off to be considered by authorities) and
- Anglesey

but also

- Arran
- Skye
- Mull
- the Hebrides
- Orkney and Shetland.

There are islands and islands! The Isle of Wight is well known as a holiday and yachting destination, but what is it like to live there in the winter? The Isle of Man has its own parliament and the TT Races as an annual event. Anglesey is where the Romans finally defeated the Druids. Skye is that romantic island off the west coast of Scotland, and the scenery of Arran is a microcosm of the scenery of Scotland. This is not enough to make your choice. Visit the island in the winter months and check the percentage of facilities that are open. Visit the island in the summer too. Is it perhaps too busy with tourists for you? Or is this just what you want? What is the ferry crossing like in the worst of the weather? How much do they charge? In the case of Skye there is a bridge, but the toll is notoriously expensive and only marginally cheaper for residents.

How big is the island? Is there sufficient social life on the island to satisfy you all year round and year after year? Is there enough custom for your business? Will you be able to fit in with the people there? This is important when there is no alternative.

Obviously your choice might take in more than one of these categories. For example, you may choose to live in a small town by the sea or a village in the hills. Or you may opt for a fishing village on an island.

Transport

Transport links are going to be essential to you in the future. If you are going to provide a specialist service, run a B & B, guest house or hotel, farm, make pottery, paint or make baskets, then either people have to get to you or you have to transport your goods. Only perhaps in the case of selling over the web will it not be so important, though you may have to send out goods by some means.

Road, rail, air and sea travel are worth looking at before you start. Houses in country areas are often advertised as being within a few miles of a motorway, especially for those within reach of a major city. Roads in country areas are often not as good as those in towns, but on the plus side they are not so busy either. And you're travelling through lovely countryside, well worth looking at.

When we were living in Wiltshire it often took me the same length of time to go to the supermarket in Devizes, 11 miles away, shop and return, as it had done in our previous existence in Richmond where I used to travel to Chiswick, only about three miles away, to shop. And it was so much more pleasant in the country!

How far would you need to travel to find the essentials of life? What about schools? Are there school buses? Where is the nearest dentist? Or doctor? Or hospital? If they were far away, would this be a concern?

Transport options

Rail links are very useful on occasion. Check for any local ticket schemes. There are concessionary tickets available if you live in the Highlands, for instance. This makes travel to Glasgow by rail (a three-and-a-half-hour journey by road) a relaxing alternative. If you intend to commute then rail travel may be essential to you. I've already mentioned the surprising fact that certain London to Penzance trains stop at Pewsey, our local Wiltshire station. Check the smaller stations on the major routes near where you want to live. It may not be every train that stops there, but as long as there is a conveniently timed one, this may be all you need. Parking is generally easier and cheaper. And a certain camaraderie often develops among the passengers at these stations. One of the Pewsey passengers frequently fell asleep well before the station, secure in the knowledge that someone would always wake him in time.

Is there a regional airport near where you want to live? Cheaper air fares mean that you can afford to fly to see friends and relations in other parts of the country and they can visit you. Tourists may choose to fly and hire a car to come to your area rather than drive long distances. Charter airlines are flying abroad from more and more regional airports every year. This can only be good news. Beware though, certain low-cost airlines are withdrawing their services on the less popular routes and you may find that your cheap flights to London or Edinburgh no longer exist.

Travel by sea may not be of interest unless you mean to live on an island. However, ferries to and from Europe increase the numbers of visitors to more remote parts of Britain. The relatively new Rosyth/Zeebrugge ferry, for example, brings European tourists directly to Scotland, making it a more attractive destination.

What next?

You've decided on the exact area or at least the part of Britain you're interested in. You know whether you want to live within reach of a town or in really remote territory. You've made up your mind whether you want to live near people or entirely on your own. What sort of house will you need for your business though? What facilities are essential to you and what more would you like to have if possible? Bricks and mortar, cob, timber, stone – farm, townhouse, cottage, hotel, tearoom, shop, country house – what will it be?

What type of property?

Consolidating your thoughts

By now you'll know the way you intend to lead your life in the future. You'll have made up your mind about the type of business you'll be running and the area you'll be living in. What do you look out for in the way of property? What sort of facilities do you need? Which are essential and which are 'nice to have'? How much ground do you want? What should be the layout of the rooms? Do you want outbuildings or a workshop? It will depend on the needs of your business mostly, but personal preference comes into it too. You will need to obtain planning permission for a 'change of use' if you are starting up a new business – for example, if you're setting up a B & B in what was a private house, or changing a workshop to an art gallery. It's wise to check first with the local planning authority to see whether they are likely to be amenable.

Let's move on to the next step now, to consider the range of possibilities available.

Hotels, guest houses, B & Bs

If you intend to buy and run a hotel, you'll be looking at hotels on the commercial property market. Buying an existing business means you're buying the 'goodwill' with the building – and paying extra for it. Studying the accounts should tell you whether the goodwill is worth the price put on it.

Be aware that you will have to comply with fire regulations, health and safety rules and disability legislation. Some of the questions you should be asking yourself and the previous owners are as follows:

- Why are the owners selling?
- Is there another pub or hotel nearby taking away trade?
- Is there any opposition in the area to the present owners or to the hotel generally. If so, why?
- Is there passing trade or would you have to rely solely on advertising?
- Are there enough bedrooms to make it a paying proposition?
- Are the facilities such as bar, dining room, beer garden etc. large and attractive enough?
- Is it close to a town or village that visitors would come to?
- Has it got some feature of the building itself or the area that you could exploit, e.g. an interesting history, resident ghost or national park nearby?
- Is there sufficient parking?
- Will it support an all-year-round business?
- Is there enough accommodation for you as the owner?
- Can you find staff in the area?
- Are there clubs, societies etc. that can be persuaded to meet regularly in the hotel?
- How do you feel about the general ambience of the hotel? Is it welcoming?

Guest houses and B & Bs are a different proposition altogether and much easier to cope with than a hotel if this is an entirely new venture for you. Some of these are purpose built and, of course, if you are buying an established business, you'll have the advantage of the goodwill. Again, check the accounts to see whether the value put on this 'asset' is an accurate one. If business has been bad, you have to feel confident you can turn things around and make a success of the venture.

Establishing the potential

Don't look at the furnishings only – though they may well be part of the business you're taking on, they will not necessarily be to your taste. Many will not have been updated for years and might be a little depressing. See beyond this and look for potential. It means of course that you are paying for these furnishings knowing that you are going to have the added expense of replacing them. This should be a consideration in the price you offer. Some questions to think about are as follows:

- How many bedrooms do you need to make this a viable proposition? Are they of a good size?
- How much work is needed to bring things up to your standards and what will it cost? Bear in mind that en-suite facilities are expected nowadays.
- How many other similar establishments are there in the vicinity?
- Is there business for all or is that why they are selling?
- Is this too remote for visitors? Will they find you if you are off the beaten track?
- If you want passing trade, is there a sign up already? You will need to seek planning permission to erect one otherwise.
- Is the area/road outside too busy and will there be too much noise?
- Will you have private accommodation that can be shut off when necessary?
- Will visitors be passing through the area (in which case there will be mostly one- or two-night lettings) or is it in a place where people will want to stay for a while?

Bear in mind that guest houses and bed and breakfasts have to comply with fire regulations and new disability legislation if they have accommodation for more than six visitors. Check with your local building control officer or planning department.

Self-catering

This is an increasingly popular market for holidaymakers within the UK. It has many advantages for the visitor and the owner. Visitors have their own space to feel relaxed in and can do what they want when they want – within reason, of course. It is usually a cheaper alternative for families with young children, but it is also an option for couples who perhaps prefer the privacy and freedom of catering for themselves. For the owner it has the advantage over a guest house of having a 'changeover' only on certain days – usually once a week during the high season. And your house can remain totally separate.

Decisions have to be made as to the sort of 'cottage' you want. Some alternatives you might think about are:

- chalet park with several chalets and usually extra facilities such as a children's play area and swimming pool;
- quieter, smaller parks with only a few chalets/lodges;
- building converted into several cottages/flats – often a large house with outbuildings;
- few, well-spaced cottages – traditional or new build;
- single cottage as part of or close to your own house.

If you're looking at the first two alternatives then you'll probably be buying an established park. If you want to expand the business in the future, it is always possible to seek planning permission for more chalets.

Many of these chalets or lodges have limited insulation and/or electrical heating and may not be so suitable for winter letting. This could be a real disadvantage as this shortens the season and the Christmas/New Year letting period is a lucrative one in many areas. You have also to consider the maintenance of the grounds and the facilities; you'll need staff to clean and prepare the chalets each week; older buildings may have to be brought up to standard with new regulations – check with the local planning department, the tourist board, the Association of Scotland's Self Caterers (ASSC) or any quality assurance agency.

You may not need to hire staff if you intend to have fewer than about five cottages; it depends how 'hands on' you are. This can save costs, especially until you're established. Single cottages are popular with people seeking peace and quiet, though as many as four cottages would be needed to make enough of a business to live on, albeit quietly! Visitors demand higher standards nowadays and if you can provide features such as en-suite bathrooms, you'll have an advantage in the market.

Getting your standards right

Make sure that your visitors have an element of privacy if you have several cottages. Each should have some designated area to sit outside and have a barbecue too – an area with garden furniture for their exclusive use. If you have children staying it is important that other guests can still have peace and quiet.

Drying rooms are essential if you are in climbing or walking territory. Open fires or stoves are very popular, particularly with winter visitors; this can be the deciding factor for a Christmas or New Year booking in many cases.

When initially looking for somewhere to convert, our intention was to choose somewhere that we could change into cottages, each with their front door onto a courtyard. Many of the houses we saw were tall, with three or more floors – suitable for conversion into flats rather than with the feel of separate cottages, albeit terraced. It depends on the style of holiday accommodation you want. It's important to realize that, with planning regulations, each cottage has to be separated from any other by a firewall. This is relatively simple when the dividing walls are vertical from ground to roof but more expensive to carry out if one cottage is partially above the other, i.e. 'stepped', or if the roof space has to be subdivided.

▦ Pottery, painting, sculpture workshops

The first decision you will have to make is whether you intend to sell your pottery, paintings etc. from your own gallery or house. If so, you can't afford to hide yourself away in some remote cottage. You'll need passing trade. This doesn't mean that you have to be in a busy area, but it will help to be somewhere visitors will come to, preferably all year round.

Will your work be appreciated? Some connection to those areas where there are already artists or sculptors would be an advantage. A known 'craft trail' will bring people to your door. Is there a village or town nearby with a gallery? Or can several of you get together and find an outlet for displaying and selling your work? You will obviously need a studio or workshop at your house. Would it be better to have a room in the house or is it necessary to have a separate building? What about the lighting? Are the windows sufficient? Is the building secure? Think about the winter and any heating necessary. Will neighbours object to your setting up in a workshop in your garden? Would this make it easier, though, to keep your home and work life separate?

Shop or gallery

Some village businesses are more popular than others. Rural post offices seem to have an uncertain future, but you could perhaps diversify into other goods to bring in the customers. Newsagents are always necessary but don't perhaps generate sufficient profit to support a family. Choosing your village carefully and studying the market could provide you with extra income providing bakery goods or expanding into a delicatessen. Those who have moved out from the city and settled in the area will appreciate being able to get their favourite cheese or wine locally. Consider specializing in some way, baking your own bread or cakes and selling these daily, for example.

Opening an art gallery is an attractive proposition. Is there a market for it though? Those on lower incomes in country areas are unlikely to be interested. Check the shops in the area – only you can tell whether you will find a market. Is there a sufficiently affluent customer base? You will need publicity too. Do you have contacts you can draw on for the grand opening? People will come from a distance if they know about you. What about those tourists? Are they the discerning type?

Again, would you be on a 'craft trail' that will bring visitors to your gallery? What about the possibility of opening a cafe in the gallery? People will feel comfortable coming in for a cup of coffee or tea and it is a good ploy to get them through the door. Is there space for a kitchen and some tables and chairs?

▓ Farms, market gardens, stables, outdoor centres, etc.

The most important feature of your new property will be the land. The land has to be fenced. Who is responsible for all the fencing on the property? A farm will have its own land, but the other activities may need to be set up by you. Check around to see whether your type of activity already exists. Will this be the 'opposition' or will the fact, say, of a number of smallholdings in existence draw you to the spot? Here the house may come as an afterthought; it will be the land that is important. Will you want greenhouses? Are they there already, and if not, will you get planning permission for them? Check for rights of way. You may be happy with ramblers coming through your property, but then again you may not. In Scotland the legislation is different; access is much more open and the right to roam is now law.

There are certain areas which are known, for example, for their market gardens and which already have a ready market in nearby towns and villages. To buy in such an established area might be a very good idea if you are new to the business. You won't have to fight for a market for your goods and hopefully you'll have help and advice from your neighbours.

Horse riding, pony trekking, outdoor activity centres all need lots of space. Are you in an area where there is land open to walkers and horses? Animals require feeding and caring for all year round. Will you have outbuildings or stables available and if not, will you get planning permission to build them (an extra expense)? And of course, you certainly want to be far from any other businesses of the same type.

Accommodating your customers

Will you be combining accommodation with riding holidays? If so, you will need to think about the number of bedrooms available in the house. Would you consider self-catering perhaps to boost income? You will need cottages or lodges for this unless you convert part of the house. If you have the land available, you will have to check the planning possibilities.

An outdoor activity centre usually has its own accommodation. Buying an established one cuts down on the expense of extra building. These centres are sometimes in large old properties – you will have fire regulations, health and safety rules and disability legislation to contend with. Hopefully, in an established business, these are already being met, but check for any new legislation you may have to follow. Are you going to live in the centre itself or will you need a separate house? You may be in remote country here. What about staff? Can you draw on local labour or will you need to accommodate them in the building?

▨ House with an office

If you are going to be writing for profit or running a business over the web or even working as a consultant, electrician, garden designer or any of a number of possibilities where your choice of home will usually make little or no difference to your business, then you're perhaps in a more fortunate position. In many ways this is an easier choice. You have more freedom and fewer restrictions on the type of house you choose and the area you want to live in. One of your main considerations, though, when buying your property will be the office space.

Some thoughts you should have are as follows:

- Is the layout of the property suitable as it stands? If not, can it be changed easily? Do you need separate access for client visits?
- Is there an office or a room you could use as one?
- Is it in a quiet part of the house?
- If you plan additional staff, will you require additional office/ workspace?
- Will it hold all the furniture, storage facilities and equipment you need?
- Are there planning and insurance implications connected with business use?

Those advertisements you see of smart offices set up under the stairs or in a corner of the sitting room are misleading. You should be able to shut the office door behind you when you leave – it is a good physical and mental barrier. You don't want the children playing or the TV to interrupt your work and having a door between your work and leisure time is beneficial to all of you. You don't have to tidy up your desk every evening either!

Action plan 5.1

In relocating to the country, you'll have some sort of picture in your mind of the house you're looking for. You may want a black and white timbered cottage, an elegant Georgian rectory or a large Victorian mansion. Whatever you choose, there are some general points worth thinking about before you make an offer. Here's a checklist to use, either when considering actual properties or to establish the type and size of property that you really need to realize your downshifting ideas:

1. Are there enough bedrooms?
2. Is the house large enough or can it be extended?
3. If you want a 'farmhouse' kitchen, is this possible?
4. If it's important, is there an Aga or Rayburn?
5. Is there sufficient head height in all the rooms and for the doorways?
6. Will your furniture fit in the rooms?
7. Are the windows large enough to let in the light and sun?
8. Is the house placed so that the garden and the main rooms will have sun most of the day?
9. Does it have a view?
10. Are there open fires or the possibility of such?
11. Are you sheltered from the prevailing winds in winter?
12. Will the previous owners be living close by, perhaps on part of the original ground? If so, are you happy with this?
13. Are any of the bedrooms through from other rooms?
14. Are there enough bathrooms?
15. Is there a large enough garden/grounds?
16. Are there mains services or will you have your own water supply and sewerage?
17. Is there a drive? Is it shared and if so, with whom? Are you responsible for its upkeep?

Check back through your responses. Do any of the negative ones identify shortfalls which might be unacceptable? Are there any compromises or redesign solutions? Make notes of any immediate thoughts which occur. Has your attitude towards the property changed (for better or worse)? Does it have the potential you need?

Some real property considerations

Many old country properties have bedrooms through bedrooms, which can be inconvenient as the children grow older and it is not always possible to change. Ceilings can be low and doorways too, especially in the attractive black and white timbered houses in the English countryside.

If in moving to the country your ideal is to have a 'country' kitchen, you will need a large room with the possibility of an Aga or a Rayburn, especially if you see this as the heart of the house. Both are expensive, but you can buy them second hand. A Rayburn will run the central heating too without a separate side unit and is more controllable if fuelled by oil or gas. Go to a showroom and get all the details to help you decide. If you want a gas cooker, check that there is mains gas in the area (not always the case). You might have to have tankered or bottled gas instead.

At one time we lived in a small cottage in a village in Scotland. It was a romantic start to our married life but what used to get me down was the fact that the sitting room was dark and we had to have the light on all day. In our present house the windows are large to let in all the light possible. Check whether the main rooms in the property face approximately south. In northern areas it is worth making the most of the sun, particularly in winter. It's not just the fact of having more light; the sun streaming in makes the house warmer too.

Sunlight and wide vistas

If you're buying in an area with mountains, beware. Some houses in the Highlands of Scotland, for instance, get no sun at all in the winter months – just when you need it most. They are overshadowed by the mountains and the sun never rises high enough in the winter to shine in through the windows. This sort of area sometimes becomes a frost pocket too, where the mist or snow lingers longer.

If one of your criteria for moving to a beautiful area of countryside is to have a view, then hold out for one. We look over a loch with mountains beyond and never get tired of sitting by the window watching the scenery. It is ever changing. Check though that there are no plans for any building development which would impact on your view.

Down to basics

We have our own water supply and sewerage system. This isn't the problem you might suppose. The septic tank requires emptying only about every three years and is not expensive compared with the price you would be paying for sewerage rates. Because we have holiday cottages we have our water inspected every year. On advice, and as a precaution, we have installed an ultra-violet unit with filter for the water which comes from a stream about two miles up the hill. This is expensive to buy but costs next to nothing to run except for the need to renew the filter and ultra-violet tube periodically. As a result our water is pure and clear with no chemicals in it.

Mains electricity is a plus though, as a generator is noisy and disturbs that peace and quiet you've achieved by relocating.

To sum up

You have made your decision now as to what sort of property you are looking for. You know what to look out for when buying. All this is driven by how you want to lead your new life. Don't rush your decision, though – you need to get it right. Property is expensive and you don't want to make a costly mistake. Even if on paper a property seems right for the business, if it doesn't 'speak' to you then don't buy it. You'll know the right one when you see it.

Your future life is going to be largely driven by your business, but you've moved to the country so that you and your family can have a better quality of life. The key to the success of your venture will be the balance you achieve between your work and your life. This is the next step you have to consider.

Balancing your life and work

We've touched on this subject already. We've considered:

- changing to a quieter, less stressful location but continuing with the same type of job;
- changing from full to part-time working to allow time to do additional work and life-related activities which you would enjoy;
- reassessing the importance and direction of your career path;
- the benefits to family life of working from or closer to home;
- your overall priorities within the 'bigger picture'.

Now's the time to really focus on what this balance means to you, and the others who may be sharing this new adventure with you.

There's a lot of talk about getting the work/life balance right within business. Much of the focus tends towards the time spent at work, with employees in the UK apparently voluntarily working longer hours than most of their continental colleagues, and some even omitting to take their full holiday complement each year. Are they willing volunteers? Is there not a slight culture of fear bred from job insecurity which discourages people from being away from their desks for too long, in case their role is seen as superfluous? In our view, the work/life balance stretches much wider than merely judging the relative hours spent at work and home. It is certainly a strong motivational force in moving towards your downshifting and relocation decisions.

Let's focus on your work/life balance priorities for a moment.

Action plan 6.1

1. Do you want to work fewer hours, even if it means a relative cut in your earnings, in order to have more quality time?
2. Would you consider doing what you're doing now – but doing it part-time – in order to develop a second job or money-earning activity which interests you?
3. Are there activities you would like to be involved in at work, or skills you would like to develop further?
4. Do you feel sometimes that your plans for progress, and the direction of your progress, are being hampered by others?
5. Considering these activities and skills, is there any potential in your life (working in the community, for example) where you could gain experience by using them?
6. Would you be happy in a self-employed situation where work and life blended together more closely and you were no longer concerned with counting the hours?
7. In your current employment, how much control do you have over your time and work allocation? If self-employed, do you feel you could manage your time better?
8. If you were balancing your work and life, would there be a danger that you might spend too much time 'having a life', at the expense of building up your business?
9. Do you sometimes feel that you're taking a very narrow view of your life and work and would like to step back to view the 'bigger picture'?
10. What is the key issue of importance to you in balancing your work and life? Is it money, fulfilment, job satisfaction, time to yourself, family involvement?

There's certainly food for thought there. Some of the latter questions are perhaps areas you might continue to address in the years to come, as your downshifting views evolve. Cutting to what perhaps is the key issue for work/life balance where you are considering downshifting and relocation, let's review the working time implications of downshifting to self-employment.

The 24/7 world of self-employment

People, whether employed or self-employed, seem to be very proud of being on the go, supposedly, for 24 hours a day, seven days a week. Apart from the evident fact that this is an unreal boast, as they would have collapsed in an exhausted heap from lack of sleep a long time ago, is it really a target which people should be striving to achieve?

One of the dangers in self-employment – especially in the early, work-hungry years when you are building up the business, and even more especially if you are working from a home base – is the fact that you never quite 'lock up the shop' and go home. There is always the temptation to pop back to the office after the evening meal to write those letters or e-mails, get the financial books in order or tackle all those other administrative tasks that you will find yourself doing in your spare time.

So, you have the potential trap in which, giving up conventional work to achieve a better work/life balance, you finish up effectively spending more of your '24/7' existence involved with work. This is especially true for public-facing situations such as hotels.

But is this broader flexibility necessarily a disadvantage? Although we are not encouraging an 'all work and no play' approach (which after all made Jack a dull boy, as the saying has it), there are several positive considerations to justify this wider self-employed involvement:

- You get the direct benefits (financial and developmental) of all your efforts.

- You can view your time more flexibly – work an evening to meet a deadline but have a morning off some other time, when work is quieter.
- Weekends are no longer weekends – have your day of rest on a Thursday (or whenever) some weeks if it suits your interests or hobbies better.
- Flexible hours and more control over what you do and when you do it will allow you to choose the best times of the day to do different tasks.
- The flexibility gives you the opportunity to have more time with your partner and family.

Making best use of your time

This last one has quite important implications in managing your work/life balance. Take writing, for example. You may have heard of authors who go down to their den in the garden and stay there until they've produced their 1,000 words for the day, at which point they switch off and watch TV. I've never managed to do it that way. Some days, I'm really productive, with words hitting the screen as quickly as my little fingers can move. At other times, I stare at the screen, my head threatening to slump forward and hit the delete button. Evidently time to do something less creative!

Kite flying

I have this theory. I tend towards thinking in the 'now' or present and planning the future, with not too much concern or even re-membrance about the past. I therefore try to spot opportunities and respond to them in what I visualize as tossing kites into the air. At any given time, I have a variety of kites flying and part of my work/life balance thinking is keeping an eye on these different opportunities. Periodically, one or other kite string needs a bit of a tug to keep it flying; periodically, one of the kites begins to soar and twist madly, requiring more of my attention; occasionally, several kites do this simultaneously, with the additional efforts necessary eating into my 'life' time for a while. However, this is balanced by the calm breezes of other times, where I can leave my kites flying on their own and enjoy myself doing the things I prefer to do.

Of course, the final element of the kite analogy means that sometimes I decide it's not worth the additional effort keeping a particular kite in the air, either temporarily or permanently. Having made the decision, I let it fall and focus on the elements of my work and life that I can progress forward.

Effective working: an attitude of mind

Having more control of your work/life balance is seen by many people as a benefit in its own right. They view the part of self-employment or self-sufficiency which allows you to make your own decisions about priorities, work loads and allocated free times as one of the key pleasures and assets.

Most people have identifiable productive and less productive times in their working day. If you are working nine to five, this can become a problem. But if you are self-employed and your work is creative, for example, you might be at your best very early in the morning, or even late at night. You can adjust your timetable to incorporate this. Where you may be involved in a variety of activities, you can allocate these to the times of your day which are most suitable – creative thought and action at the high spots; mundane but necessary chores during the low spots. And always, you have the motivation of knowing that you have the flexibility to slot your off-duty, life-enjoyment times in there as well.

When I started out on the self-employment road, we lived in an area of London and I was involved in designing and producing learning materials for clients and delivering training courses. This meant that I had times away from home and times when I was slaving over a hot computer in my home-based office. I charged per day for my time, with days divided into 3.5-hour slots. However, these could be morning, afternoon or evening, which gave me an additional degree of flexibility. I agreed these charged times with the client, ensuring not only that I was giving value for money but also that I was around working in the office when I said I was, should the client phone. I must confess that old working day habits took some time to die out before I could finally stop feeling guilty about being out 'having a life' around Richmond during the working day. My concern, I suppose, was that people might think I was unemployed rather than taking a well-earned rest!

▒ Differing balance points

Whatever self-employed downshifting activities you choose to become involved in, there are likely to be a whole range of areas of involvement, some of which you'll find more fulfilling than others. It is important, however, that you cover all the aspects in order to keep your affairs running properly. Few people get an enormous kick out of keeping their paperwork in order, but we have probably all heard of good tradespeople who have gone out of business because their tax and VAT affairs have become hopelessly disorganized.

Equally, there is a danger that when business is going well, we don't allow the time to identify new business and this can create a feast and famine, rollercoaster ride in our business affairs. Then again, we can either work too much or too long in the busy times, exhausting ourselves, or let the freedom go to our heads and become a little too relaxed towards fee-earning activities.

- If we have set up some form of creative studio, it's not enough to be producing paintings, pottery or candles. You have to market and sell them, directly or indirectly, in order to make a living.
- There is a danger that if you've set up a consultancy of some description, companies will be keen to call you in to initially discuss ideas but less keen to pay for your services.
- There is a benefit – and hoped for knock-on benefit – in offering your professional services free to the community. Keep this in perspective, however – others will be doing it while also drawing a regular income.
- One of the necessities for supporting a 'multi-kite flying' type of existence is a good filing and reference system, so that you can readily call up the documentation for any one of your different projects.
- Keep some form of 'things to do' note-taking system, so that you can vacate your mind periodically of outstanding actions.

There is little more frustrating to your partner than you thinking 'work' while out having a 'life'.

Sorting out your personal balance point

It should be apparent from the above thoughts that work/life balance is a personal thing, which you must progressively sort out to suit your own requirements. However, if working from home, remember to factor in the views and needs of your partner and family to ensure that the balance point suits their needs as well as your own. However creative you might feel in the evenings, it would be unfair to your partner and any children if you disappeared into your office each night, having spent the afternoon on the golf course.

From our experience, work/life balance is a constantly shifting scenario, affected by a range of factors including, among many other considerations:

- volume of work;
- time of year (relative to normal business volume);
- response to weather conditions;
- financial pressures;
- varying priorities and current projects.

Flexibility and selectivity

It would appear to be very important to keep an open mind in order to respond positively to these variations and not become bogged down in any particular aspect. In an ideal situation where there is enough work available, one of the benefits of running your own life and business is that you can be selective – you have the scope to choose and will have control over the ways you choose.

You can be selective about:

- when and where you work;
- the projects you become involved in;
- the clients you work for;
- the products or services you offer;

- the times of day and week you choose to work;
- times you can dedicate to family and life;
- the average split between life and work priorities;
- the skills you wish to develop;
- the working conditions you prefer;
- life aspects which you wish to develop.

Does the idea of this flexibility excite you? If so, you may well be mentally prepared for downshifting and having a greater degree of personal responsibility.

Reality check

However, it is fair to remind you that the above list was preceded by the phrase 'in an ideal situation'. We are rarely in such a position, which is why we must be flexible while still having an eye on our ultimate objectives. Initially, for example, you may have to work for some clients who are below your ideal, in order to gain both experience and income. In the early 1970s, when we were both teachers, we ran a mobile discotheque when such things were very new. Some of our early gigs were with local youth clubs, which were rather too close to our teaching activities for enjoyment, but we ultimately progressed into the Scottish hunt ball circuit, which was much more enjoyable – and lucrative!

The feast/famine aspect of self-employment referred to above is another situation which can push you towards agreeing to money-earning activities which you might otherwise refuse. Again, the need to do this will fluctuate depending on your financial situation and on the changing priorities of your particular business. Preferred styles and demand seem to fluctuate in cycles for the vast majority of work-related activities and we must flex and change with them to the best of our ability in order to maintain progress, or at worst keep our heads above water.

The buck stops

This is not to be despondent about possibilities; rather, it's being realistic. Viewing your work/life balance, you alone will be responsible for keeping the equilibrium as much as possible – there's no one else to blame.

- Not enough business? Check your marketing, advertising and product/service.
- Working too hard? Be more selective about the projects you take on.
- Spending too much time on administration? Condense, or outsource it.
- Not having enough family life? Schedule particular times and stick to them.
- Missing out on your life interests? Try to incorporate some aspects at work.
- Finding balance to be more like a see-saw? Keep working towards your goal.

Action plan 6.2

Here's a chance to make some instant responses, in order to note down some of your key downshifting priorities as they stand at the moment. It will be interesting to check back on these later, once your thoughts have consolidated a bit more.

1. How many days per week on average do I plan to work?
2. What hobby/pastime would I like to do, for relaxation?
3. Will I need extra staff or can I/we be successful in a sole trader business?
4. How would I describe the key market for the product or service I plan to provide?
5. What are the true feelings of all family members/partners involved in the move?
6. Roughly how much will I need to earn annually to live and maintain the property?

7. How do I/we plan to maintain an income stream during the quiet spells?
8. Which particular parts of my/our plans really excite me at present?
9. If having friends/colleagues is important, how will I make/maintain these contacts?
10. Are there any big question marks remaining for which I need to seek answers?

It's time to take stock of your progress and decisions so far.

The story so far

Now it's time to pause for breath, think through the points we've been considering so far and reach some decisions – it may not be right for you. Alternatively, it may be OK ultimately, but not now. Or the ideas could be really lighting your fire, big time! Here's our opportunity for a review.

This chapter consists largely of questions, revisiting key areas from our studies this far. In order to clarify in your mind what your personal way forward should be, it's important that you respond to the questions and write down your answers somewhere. We suggested earlier that you have a notebook to record your answers for future reference. This is the time to use it – or even write your answers in this book, if that doesn't offend you. You may even find, in checking back, that some of your parallel answers have changed or refined in the course of our considerations. Keep notes of these different responses – your later ideas will build on earlier ones and may even help you clarify what you really think.

▪ Where do I stand?

There were many possible reasons for downshifting set out in Chapter 2. In the action plans you were asked to identify the key factors which you thought might affect you and the key characteristics which you think make you tick. Try answering these supplementary questions, to focus more precisely.

Action plan 7.1

1. Do you wake up sometimes in the middle of the night? If you do, what do you lie thinking about?
2. Does maintaining your present home and lifestyle regularly drain your income or do you see them both as real assets, worth the investment?
3. In terms of stress, cost of living, family situations etc., has your quality of life improved or deteriorated in the past five years? Give reasons for your answer.
4. Thinking of your normal working day existence, which two activities do you find hardest to accept? What specifically would make them more bearable?
5. If there are additional significant others in your household, how do they feel about their current existence and how would they like to improve their lot? How well do these ideas fit with your own?
6. Are you more of a 'mental' or a 'physical' person? If physical, what main activities do you think you are good at? How could you apply these to earn money?
7. Could you live happily in a basic, rural atmosphere? If you think you could, which of life's luxuries would you miss most? Which could you never do without?
8. If you downshifted, would you want to give up doing your present work completely in favour of something else or might you continue with elements which you enjoy?
9. Are you a 'people person' or do you prefer working quietly on your own? Does your present work suit this preference and would your future ideas fit as well?
10 Considering all the responses above, do you think that you're ready to make a move, now or in the near future? If there are any outstanding doubts, what are they?

So, you've been considering yourself quite closely – we hope you like what you see!

Action plan 7.2

Having reviewed your answers to these questions, if there are any other points you need to check up on, make a note of them.

Applying SWOT

Do you remember the idea of using a SWOT analysis to establish whether a particular idea held potential for you? You can use this type of thinking to compare and contrast different jobs, places, skills, capabilities, anything really. It is a good way of objectively comparing like with like. Using it keeps your mind focused and on the ball.

Now's the time to use the same type of thinking to analyze yourself.

Action plan 7.3

1. What would you list as your three key strengths? Do you apply them as much – and as well – as you would like to in your present job? If you've identified a possible downshifting occupation, could you apply these strengths more success-fully? How, specifically?
2. If you can't apply all your strengths equally, which one or two are the most important for you to apply daily, or as often as possible? How could you do this?
3. If you have a partner who would be sharing your proposed new life, ask him/her what they consider your strengths to be. Do their answers match with yours?
4. What particular types of work or activities would give you the best opportunities to apply your identified strengths as widely as possible?

---

5. If your proposed plans involve a partner, how does she/he fit into the equation? Does this involve meaningful work sharing and do your plans consider their views?

6. If you're now clearer about possible occupations/activities which you could take up, how do you think you would market yourself to bring in income, especially initially?

7. In your work so far, have you always had a regular salary or income? If so, what difficulties can you foresee with a fluctuating income? Might this be a problem?

8. Are you a hands-on type of person? If so, how effective are you at keeping up with the administration, finances and documentation? What are your plans for this?

9. Having considered these different aspects of applying your main strengths (and reacting to any identified shortfalls), write your key future plan in a sentence.

10. Looking at the sentence you've written, how does it make you feel? If you're not excited, why not? Could you change anything to allow the buzz to flow?

▓ Inspiration

When we were thinking seriously about changing our life to what we're currently doing, I came across a saying in one of these inspirational books which many people buy and have by the bedside. I found a lady artist who lived locally and who produced illustrated calligraphy scrolls. She made us a beautifully illuminated copy of the saying, which I had framed and we hung it on our bedroom wall. As our plans advanced, we often quoted the words to each other. It now hangs in our porch and we still quote the words to each other periodically, to underline our vision and priorities. It's by Henry David Thoreau:

Go confidently in the direction of your dreams!
Live the life you've imagined.
As you simplify your life,
the laws of the universe will be simpler

solitude will not be solitude,
poverty will not be poverty,
nor weakness weakness.

– we hope it perhaps gives you inspiration too.

▒ The next stage

So, now that you've focused on your strengths and how to apply
them to the full, and have some ideas of the skills and talents you
may be able to bring to the fore if you downshift, what is the next
stage in the process? Should you be thinking specifically about how
you're going to earn a living, or should you be considering what
you're worth currently if you sell your present home and realign
your priorities?

To some, the ultimate downshifting is selling their high-value
property and retiring to a small cottage somewhere, living off the
proceeds for the rest of their lives. Indeed, this works for some people. There was a time around the late 1980s when the UK saw a fairly
massive clearout of middle management through voluntary redundancy and early retirement. I am aware of many managers in their
early 50s who accepted the financial package with alacrity. To some
of these, the concept of doing nothing for the rest of their lives was
a very attractive one. Although it's still working perfectly for some,
I know of others for whom the gradual undermining of feelings of
self-worth or financial stability, or both, has created problems.

If you (not the mortgage provider) have a lot of personal capital
tied up in your current property, it is obviously an important factor in the overall future equation. The days when you could buy a
Scottish estate for the price of a flat in London are probably long de-
parted, but there are certainly impressive price differentials around
the country. It's worth doing some ballpark figure calculations at a
relatively early stage in your considerations to give you a financial
handle on the viability of your overall plans. We'll discuss this in
some detail in the following chapter. Your ideas for downshifting
from employment to self-employment may be reducing your overall running costs day to day, but setting up your own business can be
quite expensive initially. You must remain in control, especially in

the early days when you might feel cash-rich from releasing your assets. If you get involved in building renovation, these assets dwindle away all too quickly.

So, earning a living and working out your worth: let's consider them both together.

Action plan 7.4

1. In round figures, how much do you think you need to earn per month in order to live comfortably? Considering your new plans, how would this change?

2. Now that you have a clearer idea of how you might be earning a living, how would you actually be earning the cash: selling items you have produced, acting as a middle man, providing services at an hourly or day rate, etc.? Have you any realistic ideas of how you would achieve your necessary targets and what you might do to influence sales in real terms?

3. If you have identified several possible skills which you might exploit, would some earn more than others? (For example, eight hours' consultancy: several hundred pounds; one hour giving therapy treatment: £20; several days producing a painting: £150.) If you were involved in a range of activities (multi-tasking), do you think you could cope with potentially earning money at different rates in this way?

4. Do you have a rough idea of the costs which might be involved in your setting up to provide the products and/or services which you have identified as your potential way forward?

5. From your awareness of property prices in your present locality, plus any current mortgage liability and other financial responsibilities which you would have to address when downshifting, how much do you reckon you would be worth at the point of buying your next property and starting your new life?

6. How aware are you of comparative property prices around the country? What do you think you could afford to buy in different areas? Do you have any proof that this is accurate?

Looking at real examples, would you need extra money to renovate or adapt the property to meet your needs? Can you afford this within your budget?

7. What is your overall plan? Are you moving completely, maintaining a flat in town to continue part-time work, having workspace on your property, buying a home but renting workspace, etc.?

8. Think your way through the key points of a mini business plan. What would you expect to earn? How much would you need to draw monthly? What capital purchases do you need to make? What are your ongoing expenses? What about staff? How does it all tie together?

9. Now that you have put some figures to your dreams, and considered the realities of downshifting and relocating, how does this change your plans (if at all)?

10. From your more detailed perspective, what would you say your two key goals are for your new work and your new way of life?

▪ Choosing your new location

OK. Now we can get down to some interesting bits (assuming that doing sums and facing up to your real worth gets a bit depressing after a while). Where would you like to live? And more to the point, where can you afford to live to have the type of life overall that would make you happy and make this whole downshifting upheaval worth the effort?

When we moved from London to Wiltshire, one of the greatest differences was the darkness at night. We lived on the edge of a tiny hamlet, with one street light visible from our property. We had a huge garage, which initially did not have any power or lights, and I remember going out with a torch to find something in the storage boxes and hearing the rustles and scratches as little creatures and birds moved around in the shadows. Quite creepy initially, but then, for the first time, we could stand outside and view the panoply of the stars without the constant sodium glow you have in towns and cities. That is a bonus, in real terms!

We now live surrounded by our own fields and woodland, with our nearest neighbours at least a mile away. We're still blessed with an uninterrupted view of the stars and don't actually think of ourselves as being particularly remote, having phased down progressively. Our many cottage guests have travelled miles from around Britain and abroad to experience these wild spaces of the Scottish Highlands. The silence and darkness are a wonderment to most, although very occasionally we do have guests who find it all a bit too different from their norm. If you're thinking of moving, you really need to travel around and test out what you enjoy and feel comfortable with. Be realistic and honest with yourself.

Action plan 7.5

1. Bearing in mind your possible downshifting plans and the potential level of your spending power, in which area(s) of the UK would you prefer to settle?
2. If you are thinking of the additional possibilities of moving abroad, have you read and consulted widely enough to be aware of the implications?
3. Are you thinking urban or rural? If rural, what level of remoteness do you think would be ideal? Have you checked out the realities of this? Any concerns?
4. Taking the particular area that you may have identified, are you aware of any property price differentials within this area which might make some locations more viable than others? Note down any key considerations.
5. Thinking about your next home, what would you say are the key 'need to haves' you would identify, which you can use to select properties worth visiting?
6. List some of the facilities' statistics (number of bedrooms, public rooms, bathrooms, storage and outhouses etc.) which you see as important check points.

7. What size of garden or land is important to you? How much time do you want to spend maintaining land? Have you spoken to someone who owns and maintains the size of land you want? What are your priorities?

8. Are there any special needs which you will have to consider in order to carry on the activities you plan? (For example, vehicle access, disability considerations, physical separation of work and living facilities, scope for technology access etc.)

9. Are there implications of special building types (thatch, timber, wattle and daub, cob, solid stone etc.) which you should be aware of before considering purchase?

10. Summarizing all these thoughts, if you are planning to move, what would you list as your current viable preferences for building, size, facilities and location?

▦ Out of the mists of confusion

You should now be reaching a point where you're clearer about your next move. This might be that you're not yet ready to downshift and relocate or that it's not for you, either now or in the future. This is OK. Better to make these decisions now and carry on as you are than to sell up in a hurry, hand in your notice and then live to regret it. If you still have strong doubts, step back and leave it for some time before perhaps considering your future afresh. You will still have your notes to refer to and you may be able to then spot where attitudes might have changed.

If you are still thinking positively about the possibilities, this is equally OK. Your goals should be clearer and your plans should be perhaps more realistic than in the early stages of considering a change.

The final consolidating thoughts that you might need to spend some time on are your particular ideas for work/life balance. You've been thinking about this in the previous chapter, so it should still be fairly fresh in your mind. One or two refining thoughts may still be in order, however.

Action plan 7.6

1.   How well do your current plans for the future tie in with your preferences for some degree of improved work/life balance? Have you any concerns?

2.   If you are seeking more time for the life aspect of your work/life balance, what specific activities do you plan to do in your enhanced time?

3.   Thinking about your new work plans, which are the key elements that will make you feel happier, helping to maintain your work/life balance even when busy?

4.   Thinking about your new location plans, which are the key aspects of your new proposed property location that will help you achieve an improved balance point?

5.   Are there any aspects of your planned work/life balance which are still unclear and might need fine tuning in order to reach an acceptable happy medium?

OK. Now that we've established many of the firm foundations, it's time to get down to the finer detail of constructing our downshifting and relocation plans.

Part Two

Establishing details and realities

Property matters: getting the calculations right

Now that you've decided on action, it's time to look at the legal, financial and planning aspects of your decision. It's essential to get these right and avoid getting carried away with the excitement of your new future. This chapter will present much of the necessary detail, as precisely as possible.

Affording the move

This is where you could quite easily get carried away. It's inspiring to look in the papers and see what you could get for your money in another part of the country. You know the area you're intending to move to now, though, so you should check what you can get for the money you want to spend.

First of all, you need to get a valuation for your present house from two or three local estate agents. This won't cost you anything. Check too whether there is a rising market in your area. If so, is it worth waiting a few months? Will it be necessary to have a mortgage on your next property? Remember, banks and building societies may not grant you a mortgage on business premises. You'll have to get a business loan unless you can separate out your business and domestic premises and get a mortgage on your home only. At first you may not be earning much, if anything, so you don't want to be paying out a large sum each month while you get the business started. Then there are the costs of the move, including:

- removal costs
- stamp duty
- estate agent's commission
- solicitor's fee
- Land Registry fee (for the search)
- survey costs
- service installation/ reconnection costs
- mail redirection costs.

Get estimates for these if you're not sure of them. Any estate agent can tell you his percentage commission. This will depend on whether he is the sole agent or not. It's possible to find out the cost of straightforward conveyancing from a solicitor. Phone up a couple of removal firms and give them an idea of distance and amount of furniture – you're only asking for an approximate figure. Survey costs are pretty standard: the estate agent will recommend a surveyor you can contact.

Property survey types

There are three types of survey, depending on specific cases.

- Valuation for mortgage purposes – the cheapest. By law all building societies are required to carry out a valuation on a property before making a mortgage offer. Although this doesn't apply to banks, most will insist on a valuation being carried out anyway. It's done with the sole purpose of determining the value of the property so that the lender can assess how much it may lend. It's not really a true survey.
- Homebuyer's survey and valuation. This is a 'proper' survey which should highlight defects or problems with the property. These can be a bargaining tool for negotiation over the price.

- Building survey – the most expensive. This provides a detailed report on the construction and condition of the property. It is a good idea for older or unusual properties.

Remember that in Scotland the system of house purchase is different (see later in this chapter) and you may need to have several surveys carried out on different houses, all adding to the expense.

Now you'll have a good idea of how much you can spend on your new property. Start looking seriously.

Looking for the ideal property

You should have an idea now of exactly how much you have available to spend on the property, including the amount you intend to borrow. It will be even better if you can find something below that limit. Suggested sources for your search are as follows:

- estate agents – some also have lists of available property updated and issued on a regular basis. Put yourself on their mailing list. Phone them weekly;
- solicitors (Scotland) – many of these have their own estate agency business. In some areas several solicitors have joined together to form groups for house purchase in a 'Solicitors' Register', usually with a 'Property Shop' and a weekly newspaper of available property;
- local papers – ask a newsagent when the property sections are published in local papers. You can get the appropriate editions sent to you;
- national papers – many of these have special property supplements on certain days;
- magazines – this tends to be the top end of the market and by the very nature of the magazine (weekly or even monthly) may be out of date by the time you see the advertisement;
- the web – an increasingly popular method. Here you can see photographs of the houses, take 360-degree virtual tours of the interior of some properties and print off details. Check the sites of the major estate agents.

▧ Planning building work

You may need to carry out building work on the property you choose. Plan carefully – you will need to get an idea of the costs involved before you put in an offer. Here a thorough survey is essential. Builders may be reluctant to give estimates for the conversion of old buildings as once work starts all sorts of hidden problems can emerge. If you insist on pinning them down, they will tend to inflate the estimate to include a contingency for the 'unknowns'.

If you intend to carry out building work, you will have to obtain planning permission first. This will usually mean that you'll have to get plans drawn up to submit to the local planning department. In Scotland this will also mean you'll need building warrants for the work. All this can take considerable time and work can't start without planning consent and the warrants. You need to cost in the fees of the surveyor or architect who draws up the plans, the charge made for planning consent and for the building warrants. Check with the local planning officer first to find out whether your plans are likely to be favourably received, i.e. whether they fit in with long-term plans for the district.

If you mean to renovate the property, the surveyor or architect is the best source of information. He can advise you about planning permission, listed building regulations, safety and structural issues and possible conservation restrictions.

Getting the balance right

In choosing your future property which is to be both your home and your place of work you'll have to balance the two aspects. There are attractive old farm houses on the market with outbuildings or barns 'ripe for development'. There are also properties with annexes or separate buildings already set up as a work space or office. These may well be more expensive than the house with undeveloped barn alongside. Think carefully before you make your choice. The property with the office already in place will probably be more expensive to buy, but consider the cost of conversion of that beautiful old barn. It looks very attractive and will give you lots of space to expand your working environment, but it will cost a great deal to bring up to standard. The roof may need to be replaced, the walls damp proofed and the inside gutted and completely restructured.

You need an idea of costs involved before you make your choice, but remember that building costs have a way of growing as the work progresses. The financial reality of this sort of work can be worrying.

Managing the project

If you engage an architect, he will offer to project manage the whole building programme. If you are carrying out major building works, this is no light task. You may feel that you want to do this yourself to save money. Fine, as long as you realize what it entails.

You need to be able to visit the site regularly to keep an eye on progress. You need to be able to cope with the different tradesmen and keep them up to the mark (if necessary) and on schedule. Builders, plumbers, electricians and decorators all have to be scheduled in smoothly and efficiently. You don't want to hear that the builders have finished their work unexpectedly early and the electrician, who should be next on the scene, has started a job somewhere else while waiting to hear from you.

Keeping control of your own project can be exciting – as long as you are confident you can do it successfully without getting over stressed. And as long as you haven't got a full-time job as well.

Contingency fund

A contingency fund should be an absolute priority for you. Whatever you decide to do, whether it is buying that house with office space set up or choosing to buy to convert or extend, at some point you will need additional funds for those unexpected works. There will always be problems you haven't thought of, situations you haven't considered and crises you could not have forecast. Set aside something for this at the beginning and ring-fence it.

Having planned for ordinary stud walls, we discovered when subdividing the building into cottages that we needed specially constructed, and more expensive, block firewalls extending into the roof space. Creating the vertical firewall between two of the new cottage units meant that we had to transfer access to one downstairs room by blocking off the existing door. The builders then had to hack through a 27-inch-thick stone wall to create a door for this bedroom, accessing into the adjacent cottage. An expensive option, but rules are rules!

Change of use

You'll have to apply for 'change of use' if you're going to be starting up a business in a building where there wasn't a business there before, e.g. converting a house to a guest house or hotel or setting up a shop or gallery in an old farm building or outhouse. It works the other way as well – changing a hotel into a private house. Again the local planning office is the place to enquire.

There are also the complications that arise in meeting disability regulations. It may be impossible to fulfil all the conditions applicable if you are converting from an older building. Some leeway is allowed for this, but check what you need to do – your architect or surveyor will know. New builds require a range of additional features.

Using your house for a bed and breakfast where you have rooms for only six guests or fewer needs no planning application.

▓ Buying the property

This is not supposed to be an informative guide to buying a property, but there are a few points to note. Buying and selling property in England, Wales and Scotland is very different.

England and Wales

In England and Wales, once you have found your property, the steps in the progress of a purchase are the following:

1.   Get a mortgage agreed in principle.
2.   Make your offer through the estate agent. There are no legal obligations at this stage.
3.   Once the offer is accepted, instruct your solicitor to proceed, making sure that exchange and completion dates are agreed. Also instruct the mortgage lender and make arrangements for a survey.
4.   The draft contract is drawn up by the seller's solicitor and sent to yours, who will make enquiries and a Land Registry search. He should also submit a search to the local authority to check any planning consents and local issues.
5.   The mortgage company will then carry out a survey.
6.   Once all searches are OK, the draft contract is approved by your solicitor.
7.   You sign the formal mortgage offer.
8.   You are ready to exchange contracts. A deposit of around 10% has to be paid by you and the completion date set.

Up until the very last moment when contracts are exchanged, the purchase is not legally binding. The seller, or indeed you, can withdraw without penalty.

Scotland

The process is very different in Scotland. The transaction will be legally binding very much sooner. Traditionally, houses were marketed by solicitors, though now there are numerous estate agencies in the country, many run by solicitors as a separate business. The steps to house purchasing are the following:

1.   Get the mortgage agreed in principle.
2.   Once you have found a house, engage a Scottish (local) solicitor and instruct him to put in a Note of Interest to the selling agent. This means you will be kept informed of any developments and given the opportunity to submit a formal legal offer.
3.   Because once an offer has been made and accepted it becomes legally binding, complete the mortgage application and get a valuation and survey carried out.

4. Ask your solicitor to submit a formal offer on your behalf. If there is a lot of interest in the house, a closing date and time will have been set and you will be expected to submit the offer by then. If no date has been set, your solicitor will submit the offer as soon as possible. Your mortgage must be in place. The offer will cover such matters as alterations and extensions carried out so that all consents and completion certificates can be asked for and checked. Any queries that your solicitor might have must be cleared up in the missives (letters to and fro) that may follow. If your purchase is a simple one, this can be cut to a minimum.

5. If the seller has several offers, he can choose whichever he wishes. The seller is not bound to accept the highest bid; he can do as he likes. This is the 'sealed bid' system which is used north of the border. It can be a very expensive way to buy a house for two main reasons.

   ● You have to get a survey done before making your bid. If you're unsuccessful, you will have to go through the whole process again with the next house, and the next. In order to get over this problem, a pilot scheme is being trialled where the seller has to provide the survey, making it available to all potential buyers.

   ● You may be making a bid well above that of the next interested party. There is no way of telling. The estate agent might give you an approximate idea, but it is only approximate. He, after all, is acting for the vendor.

6. Entry is on the date specified in the offer.

The offer system in Scotland
A word of warning here. In some places, notably Edinburgh, it is accepted that in order to have any chance of buying the property, you must offer several thousand pounds over the asking price. If you don't know the system, you don't know what to bid. Of course, the very fact of a closing date means that the seller is confident of getting a lot of interest.

The plus side of all this is that once your offer is accepted, you can be confident that the property will be yours. A chain has no significance in Scotland as you are legally bound anyway and have to come up with the price on the set day. Nor is a deposit necessary for the same reason.

The really stressful situation arises where you are selling a house in England and buying in Scotland. You have an offer in for your English property and you've made a successful bid on your Scottish property, which means you have a legally binding date by which you have to come up with money. Your English sale could still fall through, leaving you with a real problem.

There are certain properties in Scotland that are sold at a fixed price and here you have the best of both worlds. You know the price, there is no 'sealed bid' system and you have a legally fixed entry date as soon as your offer is accepted. This is the case with new houses or sometimes with major conversions. It is possible, though, to find a property where the vendor wants to sell quickly. He or she may not want to go through the extended 'sealed bid' system and is happy to have the whole matter settled as soon as possible.

Grants

If you are intending to renovate your property or to build an extension or even a new building, the costs could be high. There may also be the cost of new equipment or furnishings. However, you may qualify for a grant. You'll have to decide whether your business start-up is likely to be eligible for one and whether such a grant is worth the effort of applying for.

In order to qualify for a grant there are four main problems to overcome:

- You must be ready to put up some of your own money. Grants usually cover only 15–50% of the total money necessary to set up the business.
- Grants are available only for certain businesses.
- You will have to draw up a business plan. You may have one already if you have applied for a business loan from your bank.
- There are always restrictions set by the grant scheme. Are you willing to abide by these? They usually mean that the business must be a start-up and not one which is already in progress, the business must be of the kind supported by the grant provider (i.e. seen as achieving the objectives of the agency or department) and you may well have to pay for membership of certain organizations or schemes supported by or of interest to the provider.

Grants are sometimes dependent on the location in which you will be living and working. In rural areas, certain types of business, such as the tourism industry, crafts, agriculture or anything to do with environmental issues, are often targeted for special funding. Businesses which boost employment are of particular interest to grant providers in areas of high unemployment. On the other hand, starting a business in a relatively wealthy part of the country is unlikely to qualify for a grant.

Possible contacts for grant schemes are:

- your local Business Link or other business support agency;
- sources of free information such as your bank, your trade organization or regional development agency;
- local enterprise councils.

Completing the forms

Once you have decided on the grant you're interested in you will have to submit a proposal. This usually means drawing up a detailed project description with an explanation of the potential benefits the business will offer. These must fit in with the aims of the grant scheme. You will also need a detailed work plan with full costings and will have to show how your background and expertise will make the business a success.

Once your application is accepted you will have to keep records of where the money is being used. Grants are usually handed over according to an agreed schedule, perhaps in instalments at fixed periods or in arrears with proof of actual expenditure. There may be a final audit before you're given the last payment.

Moving on

You've sold your old house now and made any financial decisions with regard to grants, loans or mortgages. You have moved to your new home and are about to start on the real adventure of living and working in the new environment. This is to be both your home and your office, at least part of the time. How do you go about setting it up? What do you need in the way of layout, space, communications, equipment and furnishings for that office? What is going to be your first priority when you've moved in? How will you get on with your new neighbours in this very different life where you are 'around the neighbourhood' for most of the day perhaps?

It's time to think specifics.

Working from home

Working from home is becoming the ideal for many people – a 2003 report stated that more than 50% of the incomers to one particular area in Wales were intending to work from home. As readers of this book on downshifting, you probably have similar plans – not dreams now, you're thinking positive! As someone who has done it since 1985, first in London, then Wiltshire and now in the Scottish Highlands, I can commend it highly, but there are some considerations we must take on board. Let's review these now, in some detail.

▨ Working from home successfully

Working from home involves:

- establishing a workspace separate from your living space;
- designing or acquiring the facilities to help you work efficiently;
- keeping on top of your paperwork by having and using a system;
- being firm with yourself in setting and sticking to a work schedule;
- being equally firm in switching off and maintaining a domestic life;

- acquiring (and learning how to operate) the necessary technology;
- building up a range of local suppliers and tradespeople you can trust;
- identifying your different roles and maintaining (or delegating) them.

Let's consider the implications of each.

Establishing a workspace

You really need to be able to close the door on your workspace and walk away from it. If you have children, whatever their age, you equally want to have a space which can be decreed out of bounds if you want. You need to be able to concentrate when you're in work mode, so you'll have to think carefully about arrangements if you have young children around. It's also valuable to be able to shut out family pets if there's any danger that they might hit the delete button with their paw or get their tail caught in your lathe, potter's wheel or other equipment.

Then there's the question of whether clients will be coming to visit you. Where this is fairly infrequent, it can be acceptable to hold your meeting in the sitting or dining room. For consultancy types of work, the visiting client will expect you to have a functional office, even though you might choose to meet him in your dining room (your version of the 'boardroom'). Have your materials and paperwork to hand and dress professionally. If necessary, excuse yourself and go to your office to get additional materials – it reinforces the fact that you have one.

Your workspace may be more workshop than office, in which case you'll want to keep it separate to cut down on noise and dust entering your living space. Each situation will have slightly different requirements, but in all cases you will have some set-up which allows you to keep your business affairs separate and in order.

Take advice on health and safety issues – it's best to keep visitors out of any area which involves working equipment (your insurance may stipulate that anyway) and these visitors will include family members. Don't get careless just because you're working at home. Business rules still apply.

Designing or acquiring the facilities

If you've already worked as an employee doing similar work, you should be fairly clear about the facilities you'll require, from the absolute necessities through to the total luxuries. Let's focus on office space for a start.

If you're planning to work as a consultant, writer, designer or in some other activity which is largely thinking/writing/communicating, this is likely to be your entire work space. If you're involved in activities which require more of a workshop environment, or work out and about, running a market garden, holiday cottage business or estate, you should still have a separate, although smaller office area to allow you to keep your paperwork under control.

So, what do you need in your office space? You'll need:

- a desk with enough space for your computer, phone and writing room;
- a comfortable chair;
- suitable lighting;
- filing and storage cabinets or cupboards;
- book shelves or, preferably, closable cupboards;
- table or workshelf space to spread work out (dependent on your job);
- technological equipment (expanded in a later section);
- potentially, a sitting area for thinking/meeting clients.

Additional facilities will be important to individuals – heaters, if a warm atmosphere helps your concentration, and a music system, for similar or creative reasons. Clock, calendar, inspirational or motivational picture, large pot plant, kettle – it's up to you.

When designing your room layout, you may be in the situation where you can specify the location of power and communication sockets. To avoid trailing cables, it's an idea to have at least one double socket on each wall where you are likely to install equipment.

Your phone socket and any additional internet/fax link-ups you may have should be accessible from your desk. Basically, if you need to use any piece of equipment or facility on a regular basis, it should be available and ready for use in your office. The key tools of your trade should take priority place.

If you need a more practical workshop arrangement to carry out your vocation, the positioning of equipment, storage for raw materials, tools and accessories should again be arranged for most convenient use. Where your work will create dust or fumes, consider the need for extractor fans. The positioning of power take-off points and sockets will also be important. As we've already mentioned, try to have a separate, clean area for your office administration, to maintain a positive, professional standard and appearance.

Action plan 9.1

Use a separate piece of paper for this exercise – graph paper is best. For the particular work you intend to pursue in your new life, sketch out the requirements you will have for your work and/or office space as a floor plan. If you are aware of the room layouts of the property you will be moving to, you can plan the relative positioning of the different items. Include as many of the requirements regarding room layout, sockets, general equipment and so on that you see as important. Visualize how you will move around the equipped and furnished room.

Keeping on top of your paperwork

Administration – or lack of it – has been the downfall of many a self-employed tradesman. Compared with just 20 years ago, we seem to have become burdened with ever-increasing amounts of paperwork. Most of it is not too complex – it's more a case of having a system and applying it consistently and constantly.

Remember, bigger companies have full-time admin departments. To you, it's part of a wider job, but you must keep on top of it. You'll be aware of the need to get, keep and file receipts for all your purchases which you can claim against the business. File them regularly, preferably on the day you receive them, because if you lose them you can't claim against them. Where your total receipts are limited, it helps if you briefly note details of each numbered document on a front sheet. If you're multi-tasking with more than one business operating out of the same office, try to keep the documentation for each business separate. For things like receipts, you can obviously claim only once against each receipt for tax purposes (for your petrol, for example). In this case, it's a matter of sharing the bills/receipts between the different business books or charging different percentages relative to work completed.

As business develops, you'll find yourself with more and more active files of work in hand and maintaining and prioritizing the flow of these jobs becomes increasingly difficult. Again a simple tool to use here is a 'things to do' list. This is another simple administrative device, which can give great satisfaction when you tick completed items. You don't need any fancy personal planner system; a sheet of paper will do. Simple as it may seem, maintaining a 'things to do' list helps you keep on top of the job and appear professional to the people who count – both your staff and your customers.

Setting and sticking to a work schedule

We mentioned earlier about being able to physically close the door on your workplace and have a life. Increasingly, companies are allowing members of staff to work from home for a percentage of their time, although this mysteriously leans towards more senior management, with Friday being a popular day. You might therefore have already had some experience of maintaining the regularity of a business day while home-based.

If planning to work from your office on some form of consultancy-type work, you may be costing this out to the client on a daily basis. If you're working professionally, this will encourage you to put in a full seven-hour-plus day (although of course it doesn't have to be nine to five). Don't be tempted down the 24/7 route – it's totally unnecessary, in our opinion. You have flexibility over your working day – have an hour off in the afternoon and work into the evening a bit to compensate. After all, you are the boss!

In many jobs, you can work more flexibly still where you're making your money from the output rather than charging by time. One of the beauties of being self-employed is that with a higher day rate or potential earnings, you don't have to work all week to earn enough. It may take some time to come to terms with this concept if you've spent years as an employee but, once achieved, it allows you to enjoy your quieter times without worrying financially.

In our self-catering cottage business, our busy day is change-over day on Saturday. Once the new guests have arrived and have been settled in, we can concentrate on administration, booking and marketing matters, which still leaves plenty of free time in between. Take some time out – pause for a stretch, a short 'thinking break', a cup of something, even a quick stroll round the garden – they all help you to work more effectively during your active, creative periods. Don't feel guilty, just think of all the interruptions you had when you were employed – and how many of them came at the wrong times, when you were in the middle of a creative phase.

With an awareness of your average working day and its expected output, you can gauge whether you have produced enough to personally declare your working day a productive success. You might create milestones for yourself – produce three turned pots, write ten pages of a business report, draft an outline design for a client's home extension, for example. If you do, you'll then be able to monitor how effective you've been. As a general observation, self-employed people tend to work longer rather than shorter days overall. The concern therefore is perhaps more regarding the alternative viewpoint: ring-fencing time for normal living.

Maintaining a domestic life

With our increased level of flexibility, we can for example include a visit to the cinema after a business meeting in town. You could take a break from work for half an hour to play with the children or dogs, progress some of the community activities you've found time to be involved with or sit with a drink and have a chat with your partner. Somehow, it makes the living that bit more delicious when you are able to do it while others are out there working.

I guess the issue we need to focus on here is the downshifting rather than your new self-employed existence. It's natural for someone setting up a new business to perhaps spend an excessive number of hours working while building it up. However, we're in the business of downshifting and one of the implicit things associated with this should be slowing down your working life a couple of notches. Find the time to live a little. Think about your family and those sharing your life aspect – and spend some quality time with them.

Work out what work/life balance really means to you. This will give you more direct control over the times when you work – and when you don't. Keep refining and revising that balance until you find something that suits.

Acquiring the necessary technology

The internet has revolutionized communication, both business and personal, and it's important that you use the various facilities to the full. Broadband access is still patchy nationally but improving, and will extend the features you can incorporate. If your business will expand through thinking globally, an interactive website is another must – just make sure you keep it up to date and refreshed.

ICT specialists often say that your average computer user (that's us, folks!) uses only a fraction of the equipment's capabilities. While I don't believe in using technology just for the sake of it, do take time to make yourself aware of the scope available. In addition, mobile phones have had an immense impact on the way small companies can do business, especially if your work takes you away from your home base and you don't have anyone to answer your conventional, land-line phone.

The office copier of ten years ago has become an integrated multifunctional machine, while reducing in price fairly dramatically over the same period. One machine can now act as computer printer, scanner, copier and fax, although if you're involved in a lot of bulk copying, it may still be worth considering a dedicated copier. Also pay close attention to the cost of the ink cartridges and printer supplies – and whether you buy colour cartridges singly or as a three-colour composite unit – when selecting your equipment. You could be seduced into buying a piece of kit because it's cheap, only to find that the recurring inflated costs of the supplies soon cancel out any apparent savings.

Even telephones have advanced greatly over recent years. Digital systems with base units and remote pre-registered handsets can be used in separate locations around your property, reducing the need for additional wiring. Basically, it's a case of sitting down and working out what your priorities are in terms of both equipment and facilities. It can be stated fairly confidently nowadays that the technology is available in a near perfect permutation to satisfy your particular business needs.

Building up a range of local suppliers

If you're relocating to a new area, it will take time to discover the range of suppliers and related trades which you'll require in order to carry out your new business. If you're living in a relatively remote area, with the nearest major town or city many miles away, it makes it that bit harder.

It is likely that many of your potential suppliers are small to medium enterprises (SMEs) where you can still go along and talk to the guy who actually does the work and knows the fine detail about the job. Somehow, people tend to have more time to talk in country areas. Go with the flow – not only will you cement relationships which will be helpful in the future, you'll also find solutions to many of your unanswered questions if you also listen.

Living in more remote areas, you'll soon realize the benefits of the various catalogue companies which deliver services and products direct to your door. These cover business supplies as well as clothing and domestic equipment. The promised next day-service drifts a little when you live in these areas of the country using subcontracted local carrier companies, but it's still a wonderful service.

There's another point to bear in mind when building up your local network of business relationships. People in small communities talk to each other – there's very little that you do that will not be observed and passed around the village before nightfall! Develop a reputation for being a fast payer of bills received for services rendered by these local companies. It will pay dividends when you finally need that emergency call-out.

Identifying your different roles

As we've already said, if you're working from home as a very small business, you'll probably be involved in a wide range of activities. One of the problems which you have to get to grips with is seeing ahead and keeping everything moving forward. However busy you are at completing the necessary work for today, you should always be thinking ahead towards future work. If you don't have a next contract, what are you doing *now* to set up the next piece of work? Short gaps between work are OK, but long gaps represent no income while you'll still have the monthly outgoings to meet. That's a real recipe for stress.

Being aware of the different elements of the job and how well you can cope with them will help you make further judgements of your level of competency in the different roles. This allows you to identify the areas where you really would be better to delegate or outsource. There's no failure in that. Instead, spend the time doing what you are good at; earn the extra money and then use it to buy in the specialist services you require. Unless it's a unique, expensive service, you'll probably finish up paying out less than you earned in the equivalent time – and get a better result.

Where do we stand?

So we have both the facilities and the people sides of setting up in your new business. We're working on the general assumption that your move has probably involved a shift from urban to rural existence. We've underlined the fact that there are different ways of doing things out in the country, with variations in diverse country areas. Some areas have a stronger aversion to incomers than others; some have a greater '*mañana*' attitude; some are very dependent on tourism and visitors, with the implications on seasonal trade; some have become heavily grant-dependent from EU funding, which tends to have a negative effect on the entrepreneurial spirit.

As well as coming to terms with the human relations side of moving to the countryside, there are many physical, building-related differences which you need to be aware of, such as septic tanks, private water supplies and potential power cuts. It's time to consider some of these.

Understanding your property

One of the key differences when you relocate to the country is that you'll become closer to the workings of your property, whether you like it or not. There are, of course, degrees of rural living, just as there are degrees of involvement in owning an urban property. If you are currently a flat owner, you may be hit by an annual maintenance charge but not get too involved in the ins and outs of how your plumbing works or whether the roof leaks. It's less than likely that you will be too concerned with what happens to your sewage, unless you happen to get a blockage within your own property. Otherwise, you lift the phone and gain the benefits of paying your charges, as well as water and sewerage rates. In winter, if the pavements are icy, you expect the council to do something about it.

This chapter will review some of the details of being a rural property owner and highlight some of the key considerations of which you must be clearly aware.

▪ Getting in touch with the finer detail

Your planned relocation might be from town to village, in which case much of this infrastructure will still be in place, albeit in a more minimalist way. If you're moving from flat to detached house, you will be almost bound to become more involved in maintaining the fabric of the property. You'll get into the way of looking at the roof periodically, for example, to check there are no slipped or fallen tiles or slates. As one-time owners of what was billed "the largest thatched manor house in Wiltshire", we would voice caution if your dream is to take on an old thatched property, especially if downshifting will limit your ongoing income. A thatched roof is picturesque but creates a regular drain on resources, due to the need for annual maintenance or a total re-thatch every 20 years or so.

If your relocation is to a single, isolated property, there are added points to note. Where we live at the moment, our nearest neighbours are almost a mile away. We like this, but some people would be fazed by the isolation. Guests to our self-catering cottages tend to love the silence, although some acknowledge that it would be too much for permanent living. Most, like us, see it as a real benefit. This is also true regarding the level of darkness. Street lighting in small villages, especially if positioned away from trunk roads, is very restricted. With isolated properties, lighting is present only if you provide it. A wide range of automatic floodlights with 'magic eye' PIR sensors is available, allowing lighting which is activated by movement. Once again, you will have to service them when the lamps fail or the sensor does not respond correctly. Progressively, if you move into more isolated living, there are fewer 'theys' to respond to your problems (as in 'what are they going to do about it?'). In many situations, you are the sole 'they'.

Doing your research

It bears repeating that, now you're thinking seriously about relocating – and have probably shortlisted a few possible areas and degrees of isolation – you should go and stay a night in these areas at different times of the year. Consider aspects such as isolation, darkness, reduced services, journey time to reach specialist shops, ability to park in the tourist season – you must be conscious of as many of the pros and cons as possible. Keep an open mind and think objectively – you really are moving towards making a life-changing decision. For financial and other reasons, you probably won't be able to turn back the clock if you regret your move in a year or two, so now's the time to check that your preferred relocation plans stand up to scrutiny. Mind you, it's not whether you relocate, it's just making sure you choose the best location for you.

Some thoughts on keeping warm

In remote areas, your central heating is likely to use either tankered oil or gas. In winter, cold spells can call heavily on fuel use, requiring regular monitoring of tank levels. This is surprisingly easy to forget if you've been used to mains gas supplies for years. Discovering that your fuel tank level is dangerously low when the weather is bad and roads are dodgy is not a good idea. You can guarantee that you are not alone in needing this last-minute fuel delivery, raising stress levels as you try to guess whether the tanker will arrive before the tank runs dry. Taking out an automatic top-up contract is the solution here. You may sometimes find yourself having to pay for fuel when money is tight and you would probably have allowed the levels to reduce, given the choice. However, it does mean that you should always have fuel to last over a longer cold snap when road access for tanker lorries may be poor. I also have it on good authority from several drivers that householders with these top-up contracts get preferential treatment in an emergency, which certainly brings added peace of mind.

There is currently some interest in heating systems fuelled by sustainable sources such as wood chippings (also known as 'biomass'). Although this perhaps lends itself to larger community projects, there certainly is potential for domestic heating using this type of system. As the number of suppliers of different grades of woodchip product increases, this is a possibility that you should consider if you are going for a major redesign of your heating system or planning a new-build. Wind, water, solar and photo-electric power are all potential sources, depending on your location and the degree to which you wish to (or have to) be self-sufficient. Your Local Enterprise Company will probably have a special department supporting these initiatives. Talk to them about the possibilities – there might even be grants available to help you install a system if your overall plans involve new business and employment.

You may be lucky enough to have an open fire or stove in your chosen property. If you do, ensure that it works properly as there is nothing quite like sitting in front of a real fire during those winter evenings. All our cottages have either an open fire or multi-fuel stove and this is definitely one of the magnets which draws visitors. We've had guests lighting the fire in the middle of summer, just to have the effect of a living fire in the grate. Although we now have our own woodland and timber source, it's not normally as easy to access free timber in the country as urban dwellers imagine. So, running even log fires can involve expense or a fair degree of effort in converting the tree in the wood to the split log on the hearth. If you live in a Forestry Commission area where timber-felling operations are in progress, you can buy a licence for a fairly nominal amount which allows you to scavenge fallen timber (but not use a chainsaw on site unless you are impressively qualified). Mixing logs and coal, which you can still use in many rural areas not within smokeless zones, gives the best heart to your open fire or multi-fuel stove. Enjoy!

The 'night soil' question

Which brings us less than neatly on to septic tanks. When we moved from London to Wiltshire, the house particulars stated that the property was on mains water and sewerage. After living there a few weeks, I was puzzled by the presence of a number of manhole covers on the rear lawn. Checking with a neighbour, I discovered that we did in fact have our own septic tank system, and a traditional brick-built one into the bargain. Having little idea how these worked, my initial worries were allayed by a visit from a wonderful guy who ran the local business emptying septic tanks. Chain smoking (for understandable reasons), he talked me through the complete operation, opening manholes and enthusing about the quality of the system and how well it was working. Rest easy, they really are normally very little problem and need emptying only about every three years. I remember a visit to the local retired major one morning which co-incided with his septic tank overflowing in his back courtyard – but then, he had forgotten all about it and hadn't had it emptied in the 21 years he'd lived there!

Modern septic tanks come ready made and look very much like a giant onion with the stalk left on. These are buried into the ground with the manhole cover at the top of the neck (stalk). They operate using a gradual filtered purification process, either directly by membrane or through a sequence of tanks in bigger systems. Thus the system progressively releases the cleared liquids, retaining the solids – I'll leave the rest to your imagination! If working properly, they don't smell and the only time you'll really be aware of their existence is the day they're emptied (which takes about an hour). Visit distant friends that day!

The joys of having no water rates

In our present home, we have not only our own septic tank system but also a private water supply. This is probably the side of our building infrastructure which gives me most concern, although this is partly due to the fact that I feel responsible for providing hot baths and drinking water not only for ourselves but for our paying guests in the cottages, supplied by the same supply tanks. Our tanks are fed by streams (in some areas, water supplies are pumped (or rise naturally) from underground aquifers). Potential problem times are in the height of summer, when the sources are more likely to dry up, and in the depths of winter, when water supplies and pipes can freeze.

Although low key, there is ongoing maintenance such as keeping the filters and pipes clear, but this is normally more than compensated for by the smug pleasure of not having to pay water rates. The inclusion of an ultra-violet disinfector which zaps any bacteria which may pass through the pipework gives peace of mind that your water quality is good, as well as lacking the chemical additives which mains supply water often has. In areas where many homes are fed by private water supplies, you will find that there is a local contractor who installs the pipework and tanks and who will come to your aid if you have problems or need the system explained. Find out who he is when you settle in rather than leaving it until the middle of winter, when you can't locate your stopcock (or 'toby' as it is referred to in some areas).

Overall, having your own system is quite interesting (if you like pottering with things and DIY) and, over our years as house owners, we've had more problems caused by water board maintenance when we lived in properties on mains systems than currently with our private supply.

The power and the glory

Another urban image of country living is that of regular power cuts and enforced living by candle light. This is a myth, in our experience. Although you should certainly be ready for power failures by having torches and a camping gas stove, you shouldn't need to use them very often. If there are major storms, power failure caused by transmission lines coming down can affect electrical supplies anywhere, in towns as well as rural communities, and our experiences of local response to sorting out problems in various locations in both Scotland and England have been impressively and consistently good.

So, the general transmission of power to your property, unless you're really remote, can be taken as read. In fact, it's only when you do have a power cut that you realize both the extent to which you take electricity for granted and the degree of dependence you have on it. Many areas of work, such as writing, architecture, practical art and handicrafts, rely on electricity due to our increasing dependence on computers or mechanical tools. If the power does fail, you can no longer carry on your profession - which is a wonderful excuse to get the fire going, light a candle or two, brew up on the camping stove and have a fine evening dozing by the fireside. It is almost a disappointment when the lights come back on again!

If you choose to live in a really remote area, you may have to rely on a generator. As well as the ongoing background noise, there is the mechanical responsibility of keeping it running, which is not for the faint hearted. If you are thinking of running a business which involves high-wattage equipment, you must ensure that your generators are more than adequate for the job. Running power lines to the nearest point in the grid system can be an expensive option – if you are considering a property which is not on mains power, review these various implications carefully. As an example, we knew a lady who ran a small cafeteria in a remote area of the west coast. The property had its own private water supply. Because it provided teas and coffees to the general public, the council health department insisted that the water supply required disinfection. This involved an electrically powered UV tube, operating 24 hours a day, to ensure that all water entering the property was free of bacteria. This in turn involved the generator running constantly – both expensive and noisy. The small cafeteria is now closed and you can't buy a cup of coffee within a 25-mile radius.

Getting to know your consumer unit

Another tip on the electricity front is to get to know your system, especially the fuse box. This is equally true wherever you live – you need to know what to do before you first experience being plunged into darkness. Modern fuse boxes have MCBs (miniature circuit breakers) rather than fuses. These are little switches which trip off rather than blow a fuse wire when an appliance or light bulb fuses so can be quickly switched back on once the problem has been identified. MCBs tend to be more sensitive than the old fuses, so you can find the system trips out even if a single light bulb blows, which can be a nuisance at times. If the property you buy still has an old-style fuse box, it is surprisingly easy to get this upgraded to a modern consumer unit with MCBs, without necessarily involving any rewiring.

An additional safety device which will be included in your new consumer unit is called an earth trip or RCD. This will switch out the related power ring circuit if it contains a faulty appliance which is leaking current to earth. Otherwise, this could give you an electric shock if you touch it, so the RCD is a valuable additional safety device.

If your electrical system is something of a mystery to you, get an electrician to check it over and explain its workings and suggest any upgrades which may be a benefit.

▧ Building up the contacts

As we said earlier, it is important that you develop a portfolio of tradesmen that you can call out in an emergency or to do a little job in your foreseeable future. The more remote you are from the operational centres, the harder it will be for you to get these tradesmen to visit, especially to give you estimates. They're all very busy; in fact, any readers in the building trade who fancy a bit of a downshift to the more relaxed country way of doing things are guaranteed to be able to get enough work, if you can fit in with the local ways!

Depending on your range of skills and abilities, you will be able to sort out your particular tradesmen priorities. Plumbing is my key blind spot, so we tend to use one plumber for all our development work (and grit our teeth and pay his transport charges with a smile) so that we can expect a more or less instant response from him when that emergency finally comes. If you can find a general builder who can turn his hand to a range of skills, from carpentry to bricklaying, treat him with kid gloves – he is indeed a treasure. Above all, bearing in mind that it will be difficult to get instant emergency response (often in stormy or freezing weather when many people experience emergencies at the same time), get into the habit of checking over your property and catching problems early. Replacing a cracked toilet cistern now, for example, will prevent the flooded bathroom and the collapsed ceiling below during that sudden February frost.

Getting in and keeping out

Owning a country property can also mean that you have access drives and boundary fencing to consider. Tarmacadam is surprisingly expensive – and beware the knock on the door from some guy with an old lorry who just happens to have half a load of tarmac left and has noticed that your drive has potholes. Whoever you use, always get a quote for the complete job (some contractors will try to quote an open-ended cost per square metre, which seems quite reasonable until you discover how many square metres of tarmac they have laid) and watch them doing the job to check on the uniformity of the thickness. Check for any cracks at the edges after rolling – water getting in these and then freezing can break up your nice new drive in record time.

You will probably find there is less stress involved in land ownership in the country. Whereas urban neighbours have on occasion literally fought to the death over disputed ownership of tiny strips of land, rural lines of demarcation are usually more flexible. When discussing your purchase with your solicitor, check carefully on the property deeds to establish exactly the land which is included. You may even find that some of this is outside your boundary fence, a legacy from when contractors came to replace old fences and took a new (and easier) line while sinking the posts. In their eyes, leaving the old tumble-down fence means that your boundary line is still intact, even though they have created a 'no-man's land' area between old and new. If this situation ever occurs for you, just remember: it's your land and you're paying for the fencing bill, so stick to your guns if you think it's important, however rocky the area looks and however difficult it might be for them to dig post holes.

The enclosure act

As with tarmac, fencing is quite expensive when you get a full quote for the job. Insist on this as fencers too will quote by the metre length – it's only when you discover the total length and the extras for gates, additional strainer posts and so on that the final amount hits you. However, when you have spent time periodically patching rusted and rotten netting and supporting worn fence posts, there's something rather wonderful about getting a brand new length of fencing installed.

Still on the fencing front, watch out for the additional costs sometimes involved if you are considering the purchase of a property which is part of a farm or estate. In these situations, you may find that part of the agreement is that you (the purchaser) are liable for fencing off the designated area you are purchasing. In the excitement of completing on your dream property, you may accept this without appreciating how much it will cost. Get a quote so that you are at least aware of the extra expense which will become due just at the point when you are recovering from all the other outlays involved in property purchase.

Some rural properties may come with several acres of land, which is a wonderful bonus, but once again it does involve ownership responsibilities. Spending regular time and effort in cutting grass and maintaining borders in a large garden may be your lifelong ambition – or it may increasingly become a millstone round your neck as you struggle to keep up with the weeds. Larger properties may have fields or paddocks which require less effort (but more fence maintenance) and if you have mature trees near public access roads, you have to keep an eye on their soundness in case any blow down in a storm. If the council turns out to remove one of your trees which has blown down over the road, you'll be hit with a hefty bill for the service. If you have streams on your property, again you have to keep an eye on the water courses to ensure that they don't block and flood property belonging to others.

But don't be put off by all these areas of responsibility – they're not doom and gloom, it's just that you should be aware that they come with the ownership. We currently own a property with 36 acres of garden, fields, woodland and loch frontage and we truly consider it a great honour being guardians of this landscape.

Reaching a happy understanding

In summary, what we have been trying to underline here is the range of responsibilities involved in owning a rural property, especially one with land attached. If you get to know the ins and outs of how your building and its services function, and are aware of the various people and services which are available to support you in maintaining operations, you can keep on top of the job. Not only will regular checking and minor maintenance keep the property functioning correctly, you will be ready for the minor or major problems when they do occur. As the old postman used to say to me periodically, a slate on the roof's worth twenty pence, but if it's fallen on the ground, it costs twenty pounds!

Owning a rural property, especially one with some land to call your own, is a pleasure and indeed an honour. Keeping a watchful and understanding eye on it will make sure that it remains so.

Business plans, budgets and cash flow

You are by now confident of the ins and outs of living the dream with regard to the property and the area. What about the financial side of things? Not so exciting, but it's essential to get this right. If you need finance you'll have to draw up a business plan. You should also be working to a budget, both for setting up and for the everyday running of the business. And what about cash flow? Money will be scarce at the start-up of the business and probably for some time after that. You need money to live in the meantime and also to carry out any building development necessary. Lots of aspects to view, and this is the time to face up to them.

▦ Business plans

These are not as intimidating as they sound – a good business plan will focus your mind as well as helping you get some financial support.

What sort of information do you include?

1. **Your business and your product or service.**

The background

- What is your idea or plan?
- Have you been working towards this idea for some time? How long?
- How much do you know about this type of business?
- Have you had any direct experience?
- Have you carried out any work on the new business so far?
- Who, exactly, are to be the owners of the business? You, you and your partner or is it a family venture? Are friends involved?

Your service or product

- What exactly is your service or product?
- How will it differ from those already on the market? If you want to start up a B & B business, for example, why do you think yours will be better than those already established? Why will guests choose to come to yours in preference to others in the area?
- How do you intend to develop the business in the future? If your idea is to set up a gift shop for tourists, for example, how do you see the business expanding? Will you build an extension to hold extra stock? Do you intend to set up a tearoom in conjunction with the shop one day? Will you do mail order? How will you exist when the tourists are not around?

2. **Your market and competitors.**

Who is your market?

- What sort of customer, client, guest are you aiming for? For a shop, these could be locals, tourists, bus parties or specialist buyers, for example. For holiday cottages, your 'guests' might be foreign visitors, walkers, climbers, families etc. It makes a difference to the facilities or services you'll want to provide.
- How big is this market? Can you expand it? Is there a trend? For instance, if you intend to grow organic produce, you will want to show that more people are buying organic these days. If you are intending to provide adventure holidays then you should be able to demonstrate the increasing interest in this type of holiday.
- If you've already started your business by this time or if you've perhaps done it in a small way before, what sort of return have you had? Do you already have customers lined up and waiting?

Who are your competitors?
- What are the advantages and disadvantages of your services or products over those of your competitors?
- Why will people choose to come to you? You must show that you have done your market research properly.

3. **Marketing your business.**
    - How will your prices, quality, service and experience compare? If you are making and selling goods, what are the design features or qualities that will compare well with your competitors? What about after-sales service? If you are going to run a holiday business, how will the value for money you give your guests compare with others in the market?
    - How will you actually sell to customers? By phone, through your website, by post or perhaps through an agent?
    - Do you anticipate repeat business or repeat orders? What percentage are you aiming for?
    - Are there any interested customers/clients already?
    - How will you find potential customers?
    - How and where will you advertise? In magazines, on the web, direct mail or with organizations such as the tourist board?
    - When is your projected start-up date?

4. **Management.**
    - Who are to be the managers of the business?
    - What are their strengths and how are they to overcome any shortfalls?
    - What are their backgrounds and what experience do they have?
    - Are there any business supporters – mentors etc. – to provide informal assistance?
    - Just how enthusiastic and committed are you?
    - How much time and money will you both (all) contribute?
    - How many staff will be needed? Will they be full-time, part-time or seasonal?
    - Is training required?
    - If recruiting staff, are you aware of all the legal responsibilities involved?

5. **Financial forecasts.**
   - Work out a realistic sales/income and expenditure forecast for the next three years, breaking the figures down into components – these might be months if it's a holiday business or different types of products or sales if you are selling goods.
   - Produce a cash flow forecast showing how much money you expect to be flowing into and out of your account and when. You must show that you have considered the key factors affecting cash flow – timing of sales/amounts of income and outgoings. At what time will the business be cash positive, i.e. more cash coming in than going out?
   - For each forecast list all your key assumptions: prices, sales, income, timing etc. Business Link and Enterprise Agencies will help you put together your forecasts free of charge.

6. **Financial requirements.**
   - How much finance will you want, when will you want it and in what form? You might ask for an overdraft facility from a bank and a loan, for example.
   - What will the money be used for? Will it be building work, refurbishment, purchase of machinery, materials etc.?
   - Prove that you can afford it. For instance, does your cash flow allow you to make the payments on the loan?
   - Are there costs involved in the recruitment and training of staff or possibly training the management?
   - What sort of support do you already have? Give details of your bank, accountant, architect, solicitor etc.

7. **Appendices.**
   The information here is used to support the main text of the document. It includes:
   - any cash flow tables, monthly sales/income figures etc.;
   - market research data you've referred to in the document;
   - any technical specifications or sources of outside information you've mentioned, e.g. tourist numbers in the area, tenders for building work, costings of plant, equipment or furnishings.

8. **The summary.**
   Although this summarizes your whole plan, *it goes at the beginning*. Avoid technical jargon and use it to sum up six main areas:

- your product or service and its advantages;
- the opportunity in the marketplace;
- management;
- your record to date;
- financial projections;
- financial requirements.

9.　**Presenting your document.**
- Keep it short. Include relevant material only.
- Make it professional. Give it a title page, put on a cover if possible and include a list of contents.
- Re-read it yourself. Ask a friend to read it. Does it give a good picture of your business?

▥ Cash flow

It is always difficult to estimate costs and income in a new business, but even if you're not going to ask for finance and won't be producing a business plan, you will definitely find this useful. It's only when you get down to the fine detail of expected income and probable expenditure that reality bites. We did this because we had to when we were applying for some financial help, but we're glad we did. It made us think very clearly about what we would spend the money on. And what we wouldn't!

It needn't be an over-complicated document. We drew up a five-page cash flow forecast for five financial years. Each page had a column for every month and a row for each type of income or expenditure. (Excel is a good tool to use for this.) The income was broken down by 'source'. We had three: self-catering, training workshops and arts/crafts courses.

Initially we intended to focus on building the self-catering side, with expansion into the workshops and courses at a later date. We listed the expenditure under the different things we expected to have to spend money on. These vary enormously depending on your business of course, but there are always the main ones: insurance, heating and lighting, telephone, car and travel, postage and stationery, accountancy/book-keeping, rates, advertising, bank charges and bank/building society repayments.

You will probably have to buy some fairly major items of equipment or furnishings, at least when setting up, so capital expenditure is another heading. Then of course you may have materials to buy for the business on an ongoing basis. You'll have drawings or salaries – you have to live! Be as truthful as you can and as clear sighted – underestimating what you can live on will lead to trouble early in the life of your new business.

Cash flow forecast for year to March 2005	April	May	June	etc
Income				
Self-catering	100	200	700	
Training	150	400	300	
Arts and crafts	0	0	0	
Total income	250	600	1000	
Expenditure				
Insurance	55	55	55	
Heating and lighting	80	90	70	
Telephone	21	35	30	
Car and travel	35	82	50	
Postage and stationery	20	25	30	
Etc.	200	450	550	
Total expenditure	411	737	785	
Opening balance	0	-151	-288	-73
Monthly movement	-151	-137	215	
Closing balance	-151	-288	-73	

Your opening balance for the first month of the first year is £0. Add the difference between the income and expenditure for that month (it will more than likely be negative as you may not yet be earning) and you have the monthly movement (a negative figure in the case above). Add the opening balance and the monthly movement and carry it forward to the next month as the opening balance.

The whole process then repeats itself month after month. As you earn more and more each month and keep expenditure at a reasonable level, the figures for the monthly movement and the opening balance each month should begin to improve.

The cash flow data certainly helps to focus the mind on that all-important earning power! Looking at the figures you'll see the obvious problem. You won't be earning enough to live on for the first while, let alone pay all the bills. This means you need back up – money in hand. This is where your savings come in. Unless you have some cash in reserve, perhaps from the downshifting, you're going to have a real problem.

Simple book-keeping

Book-keeping makes the paperwork easier. Keeping it up to date means you know exactly what's going on. There are several good computer packages you can use or you may prefer the traditional paper system. If you think you're going to need a computer package later on when your book-keeping gets more complicated, it's better to start with one now.

What records do you need?

You'll need to record all the money going into your business and all the money going out, not just to keep track of things but also for your tax records. You'll need to keep:

- records of sale or money paid to you – issue an invoice or receipt (keep a copy), mark the stub of your bank paying-in slip with amount, date and name or invoice number;
- receipts or invoices for everything you buy or pay for – number these in date order and keep them in a file;
- bank account statements – open a separate account for the business; ask for monthly statements;
- statements of business loan payments from your bank or building society;
- records of any cash payments made – receipts or a written record.

Cash books

You will also need a cash book of some sort to enter all this information. This can be an analysis book (with several columns on each page) or, if you're using a computer package, this will perform the same function. We use a very simple book-keeping system which is paper based as our business is not very complex and won't become more so. In the front part of the book, we have a page per month for expenditure. In the first column on the left we write the item of expenditure with the date it is paid – telephone bill, six new chairs, etc. The next two columns are headed 'account' or 'cash'. The rest of the column headings show the type of expenditure – think this one out before you start. Your accountant will help you, but some of the usual types of expenditure are advertising, postage, building/plumbing, transport, heating/lighting etc. You'll notice that each amount is entered twice, one showing how the money is paid – as cash or into our bank account – and the other under the appropriate heading.

January

		Account	Cash	Postage	Running costs	Furniture
2nd	phone bill	120.00			120.00	
7th	6 dining chairs	360.00				360.00
11th	stamps		22.50	22.50		
etc.						

With some of the receipts, particularly those for petrol, telephone, internet and heating, we charge only a percentage of the bill to the business. This makes sense as not all our car journeys, for example, are to do with our business. The percentage you charge is up to you but your accountant and the Inland Revenue have to be convinced it's the right one. At the end of the month the totals should balance - the sum of the two left-hand columns should be the same as the sum of all the others.

At the back of the book we record the money we receive. This is much simpler. Again it is in months, with the source of income (dated), whether banked or cash and which part of the business the money was for. Again at the end of each month the totals for 'banked' and 'cash' should add up to the sum of the totals for the type of business.

January

		Banked	Cash	Cottage income	Workshops	Arts & crafts
2	Jones (4 Jan) A	100.00		100.00		
5	Ellice (14 May) C	160.00		160.00		
7	Work/life bal.	500.00			500.00	
	etc.					

This is a very simple system but it has kept us going perfectly adequately for years, and probably more important, it satisfies our accountant too.

Money in the future

The basic groundwork is done and you are ready to move on. You know how to produce a business plan and a cash flow forecast, and you've thought about how you are going to 'keep the books'. It's time now to consolidate what you know and to make sure that you have thought about all the financial aspects of your new business. Have you planned well? Are you confident about setting up your new business? What about the first year? Do you know where you're going financially? And then of course there is the longer-term view. Are you prepared?

Money makes the world go round

The love and peace aspects go without saying, so let's focus some more on the money aspect. It's been a recurring theme in this book and we have just finished focusing on some of the practicalities in the previous chapter – establishing your property budget, writing your business plan, paying for development work, maintaining a cash flow and so on. If you're setting off on this downshifting journey, making your first million will not be a high priority. But you must be realistic about making ends meet. Many projects have foundered in the short term because of (let's not beat about the bush) total financial stupidity – budgeting for a £4,500 kitchen but falling in love with a £25,000 all-singing/all-dancing design which you just had to have.

Many others have collapsed in the medium to long term because people have either paid themselves too much as a wage or have been caught out by some emergency in the quieter season, business-wise, when there's little or no income around. This chapter brings you face to face with financial realities in a simple, checkpoint format. It follows logically through the development of your business, stage by stage. Read it periodically in the future to keep yourself on message (as the spin doctors would say!).

▨ Money matters – it sure does!

We'll look at this under a range of headings and timescales. You already know some of the detail – it's largely common sense and we've covered most of it at points throughout the book. Setting it out in an easily digestible form, however, will make it simpler to check back on periodically. It's important that you keep focused on this angle of your future.

So, the headings are as follows:

- Planning: what am I worth?
- Planning: what can I get/do for my money?
- Planning: have I included everything?
- Setting up: what do I really need?
- Setting up: where's my initial business?
- Setting up: what are the timescales?
- Refurbishment: how much will it cost?
- Refurbishment: have I allowed for contingencies?
- Refurbishment: how do I keep my feet on the ground?
- First year: am I ready for the teething problems?
- First year: how do I monitor cash flow?
- First year: what's my marketing strategy?
- Longer term: how do I keep ahead (or a head!)?
- Longer term: how do I budget for development?
- Longer term: how do I respond to the bell curve?

Lots of considerations, so only a few pointers for each at this stage. Think carefully about each statement. You may have to gain wider insight through reading more specialist books, attending workshops and so on. There's a lot to think about.

Planning: what am I worth?

- Be realistic about the expected value of any property you plan to sell.
- Keep your planned borrowings as low as possible – it's your main, ongoing drain.

- Remember to subtract legal and other related fees from the expected amount.
- Don't commit everything – keep aside a contingency amount for basic living.
- Write down your final available amount – and keep reminding yourself what it is.

Planning: what can I get/do for my money?

- Keep a firm grip on the maximum amount you can offer on any property.
- Use this as a bargaining tool for properties which have stuck on the market.
- Be sensible about relative urban/rural property values – do you need five bedrooms?
- Be aware of your total cost requirements for moving to/starting your new life.
- Review unnecessary extras (land, outbuildings) – perhaps they are a financial drain?

Planning: have I included everything?

- If it's a new business venture for you, talk to people who can give you advice.
- Get to know the locality, the services available and the possible shortfalls.
- Plan the transition between selling your present/moving into your new property.
- Have you found out the costs of removal, storage etc. for your location swap?
- What if new property purchase is threatened by slow sale of current property?

Setting up: what do I really need?

- Don't get carried away by apparently being cash-rich at the point of downshifting.
- Review your potential major purchases – are they really necessary?
- What image would be expected of you in order to present a professional front?
- What budget is required for your agreed list of necessities? Can you afford this?
- Do you have a contingency plan for sourcing extra cash if really necessary?

Setting up: where's my initial business?

- Have you checked out the competition in your area/market objectively?
- What particular niche are you focused on and are you aware of your 'brand'?
- Have you checked out advertising and marketing – some have long lead times?
- Do you have a plan for networking and getting your product/ service known?
- Can you offer any bargain deals etc. to make your first sales and get things moving?

Setting up: what are the timescales?

- If renovation/rebuilding is required, are you realistic about planning timescales?
- Are you aware of the principles of project planning and critical path analysis?
- With the type of work you plan, is it possible to begin trading in a phased way?
- Can you cope with the actual timescales involved in relocating and setting up?

- Have you planned a strategy for effectively maintaining movement forward?

Refurbishment: how much will it cost?

- Have you planned out in exact detail what your requirements will be?
- Will your tradespeople work to a contract or do they prefer 'time and materials'?
- With an older property, are you really aware of the condition of the building fabric?
- Do you have a list of work items to be completed, with costs against each?
- If you're relocating in a remote area, what tradespeople travel costs will be added?

Refurbishment: have I allowed for contingencies?

- With reference to the work list above, which items might 'extend' and why?
- If you need to spend more on some items, which items might you put on hold?
- If amending existing systems (e.g. plumbing), is the contract content detailed?
- Can you hold some of your intended work back as phase two, for later?
- Have your budgets included contingency amounts for essential extra works?

Refurbishment: how do I keep my feet on the ground?

- Who will be managing the project? If you, will you be on site and available?
- Do you feel confident enough to consider the options and say 'No' on occasion?

- Do you have a system in place for monitoring projected and real expenditure?
- Do you have someone to discuss things with, to prevent ideas being too extreme?
- Are you aware of the choices available so that you can select better-value options?

First year: am I ready for the teething problems?

- Are you marketing for the future as well as responding to the now?
- Are you receiving the deliveries of the stock/materials you require for business?
- Have you built a portfolio of tradespeople to respond to any breakdowns/problems?
- Do you have backup for your key items of equipment/facilities in case of failure?
- Do you have backup support in mind/arranged in case you are sick?

First year: how do I monitor cash flow?

- Are you budgeting for expenditure or buying because you need it?
- Are you still managing to file all your receipts regularly and systematically?
- Do you feel you have some control/influence over increasing your income?
- Are you managing to service any financial loan arrangements you have in place?
- Are you aware on a week-by-week basis whether you are in the black or the red?

First year: what's my marketing strategy?

- Are you clear what your key markets are? List them in order of priority.
- How much will you spend on advertising? How do you select the best sources?
- How good are your networking skills? Is it a good way of developing business?
- Will a website work for you? If so, how will you obtain a professional result?
- As well as the above ideas, in what other ways can you get your name known?

Longer term: how do I keep ahead (or a head!)?

- Are you perhaps relying too much on currently having a few good clients?
- Are you still keeping an eye on future markets as well as servicing present ones?
- Do you feel you have control of your work/life balance, with 'times out'?
- Are you still enjoying what you are doing or do you need to rationalize priorities?
- How has your priority market refined in reality since you started trading?

Longer term: how do I budget for development?

- Can you manage to save some money regularly into a contingency fund?
- Do you regularly review current facilities and identify key development needs?
- Do you use business planning to establish whether development is justifiable?
- With whom will you discuss your plans objectively to establish a way forward?

- Are you open enough to listen to alternative views and review and revise ideas?

Longer term: how do I respond to the bell curve?

- Are you aware that any business will naturally trough after reaching a peak?
- Is your priority to sell for a profit before the peak or to fight to avoid the trough?
- If the latter, what plans can you develop to expand your business market?
- Will it be better to expand existing facilities/services or replace with new ones?
- What continuing personal development will I need to keep abreast of change?

The bell curve concept

This is an interesting idea which is worth reading more about if you're intending to run your business in a professional way. Put very simply, it proposes that every business evolves through a natural life which can be represented by a graphical line following the shape of a bell. This means that the business should initially increase in terms of success to a peak point. It will then level out for a shortish period, after which time there is a natural tendency for the business to go into decline unless some dramatic changes are put in place. There are several responses to this.

The entrepreneur

Let's take the definition of entrepreneur as someone who is grooming and selling successful businesses for a profit (which is only one aspect of entrepreneurship but is perhaps the popular understanding). The skill of the entrepreneur becomes that of identifying the point where a business is still climbing towards its highest point of success on the bell curve but is reaching its most valuable, saleable point. He/she is therefore building the company, with a staff and infrastructure which does not include him/herself in the equation, thus allowing him/her (the entrepreneur) to sell up and move on with a fine profit. The implication is that the business will be purchased by another entrepreneur with new ideas, creating a new bell curve, and the business then sets off once more on its upward curve.

The long-term downshifter

We're perhaps more likely to be in the situation of setting up our business to give us a steady income for many years or until such time as we decide to sell the business as a going concern, thus creating our 'pension fund'. As this is likely to be a longer-term proposition, we should be aware that we will reach the bell curve peak point sooner or later, and be ready to respond. If we can accept that this decline is a natural state of affairs for the business and is not our fault, we should be able to take preventative action, to maintain momentum.

The decline might be caused by issues such as:

- the property fabric and furnishings needing refurbishment;
- your range of products and/or services becoming tired and dated;
- your enthusiasm weakening, creating more negative attitudes;
- your market changing, without you responding positively to this change;
- the business turning out to be too small to generate an acceptable living.

There are potential responses to each of these issues, and some cost more than others to fix.

The business as a 'cash cow'

This is the type of response to the downward turn of the curve where one accepts that the business has a limited life and the focus of attention is making as much money as possible from it in the short term, before it folds. Looking around, you'll see this happening with some businesses where assets are stripped out and sold separately, quality of fabric and facilities is fading visibly, and often services become poor as employee numbers are reduced. Although this is one response to the bell curve situation, it is not recommended.

The solutions and responses which you make will depend on how you see your future and how you want to develop your cash-earning activities. Keep an open and flexible mind towards the ways things are progressing, but be honest with yourself. As we've been underlining in this chapter and elsewhere, keep a firm grasp of how your income, outgoings and any planned development costs are stacking up, and be realistic and objective about your overall wealth. Increasing your borrowings to extend facilities makes real sense only if directly increased income can more than match the interest repayments involved. Part of downshifting is reducing the stresses and strains of life, and balancing your finances can certainly become stressful if you don't keep them under control.

So, in this chapter we've spent some time looking at a range of considerations which will become active at different points in our future downshifting life. In the next and final chapter, we will consider and respond to many of the questions people tend to ask us at meetings and seminars when reviewing whether downshifting and relocation is right for them.

Questions and answers: getting ready to go

We have posed many questions in the course of writing this book and you doubtless have many others in your head as your plans gradually evolve and develop. In meeting a wide range of people interested in the potential of downshifting and relocation, both professionally and informally (and numbers are certainly growing year on year), there are recurring questions which we tend to be asked. Putting our heads together in one of our 'Blue Water' meetings, we've come up with the following as some of the key questions, with possible responses.

1. We're moving from a large town/city to a small village. Will the locals welcome us?

The simple answer is that you have to earn the welcome and work at integrating into the community. You'll meet a whole range of attitudes and 'chips on shoulders' which are far too complex to consider in any depth here. Understand that some people will see you as comparatively rich 'townies', coming into the community and paying a sum for property which many locals may not be able to match. Although it's likely to be a local who is receiving your money, and who has set the asking price, and although it's often only outsiders like you who are willing to buy properties in need of refurbishment, these facts are often conveniently forgotten when attitudes are being aired.

It really need not be a Scottish/English/Welsh thing, unless you respond negatively to the suggestions. Tread softly. Try to bring something to the community, but even there, realize that your potentially broader experience of life may be seen as a threat to the status quo rather than as an asset. Look on it as an interesting exercise in interpersonal skills – join one or two clubs and develop some allies within the community. You can guarantee that you will be talked about behind your back, so it helps to have a few spies and allies in the various camps. Think of it as a bit of a game and don't take things too seriously or rush matters. It takes several years to become integrated into a small community – estimates vary between five and twenty-five!

2. To what extent must I have planned everything before I finally take the plunge and decide to downshift and relocate?

The immediate response to this question is 'go with your heart but use your head'. You can't think of everything, but you do need to get a strong feel for the community and area to which you're planning to relocate. Visit at different times of the year. Check out the availability of facilities and services which are important to you: is it acceptable to have a 15-mile round trip to buy a newspaper, for example? As we have underlined in several chapters, detailed planning must include a review of financial matters. This is most likely to be the medium- to long-term stumbling block, so go down that route with your eyes wide open.

Are your decisions to downshift based on alternative (income-earning) activities which you will enjoy doing or are they driven by a narrow dislike of your current work and domestic arrangements? Self-employment is a variable game, with periods of famine as well as times of feasting, so are you ready for the rollercoaster ride? Talk to someone who is self-employed and a sole trader (perhaps a current neighbour or friend – you don't have to relocate to work for yourself) and find out some of the realities. They need not be negative at all, but you should be aware of them.

If you've been an employee in other companies up to this point and are setting up in business for the first time, talk to people to find out the requirements. If you're planning to keep your new venture small and personal, without employees, it's surprisingly simple to set up in business. There are various business advisory services available, usually free, to help point you in the right direction. There are also various grants and other forms of assistance that you can pursue, although you will be required to jump through administrative and official hoops, which may or may not be acceptable to you. It's certainly worth asking.

3. I have a dream of moving to a smallholding in Wales or Scotland and becoming self-sufficient, growing organic produce. What's the best way forward?

First and foremost, do this with your eyes wide open. Self-sufficiency is very hard work and a sudden turn in the weather can render your laboriously grown fruit and vegetables useless – then what do you eat for the rest of the season? If you haven't practised growing vegetables fairly extensively in your present back garden or allotment, don't even consider selling up and moving to Wales. Even if you have got green fingers, it is safer if you can also have a back-up means of earning some money, just in case sudden frosts or insects hit your crops.

Thinking positive, however, if you can make a go of it, there are particular estate agents/property shops which specialize in properties with land. If you want to buy a croft in Scotland, get a Scottish solicitor to handle your transaction and make sure that you really are getting the agricultural 'in-bye' land as well as the cottage and immediate ground. If you're not careful, you may find that the main fields have been separated out and sold on to a local neighbouring crofter.

Check the quality of the land as well if you're hoping to grow crops. Very little of the farmland on the west coast of the Scottish Highlands is good arable soil, for example. The east coast, central areas like Morayshire and Perthshire and the southern belt have better land, but property will be more expensive. Similarly, Wales has variable quality of arable soil. Visit the areas you're thinking about and find out for real what the properties offer. Your plan to produce crops on a property with 40 acres will end in tears if the majority of these acres are scrubland, fit for rearing sheep at best.

4. Is there a good time to make the downshifting move?

There is not usually one particular time when it is best to make the move, but you have to consider circumstances. If you have children at school, the best time is in the summer holidays between primary and secondary school or just before they move into the sixth form. While this isn't always possible, it obviously isn't a good idea to downshift in a year when they are due to sit important examinations.

Most young children are very adaptable and it's up to you to reassure them. If you tell them it's going to be difficult for them, then it will be. Treat it all as an adventure and they will too. It isn't so easy for older children, but again, emphasize the positive side of the new life while trying to answer their concerns.

We intended to make the move once both our children had finished school but in the end we just couldn't wait that long. We moved from London to Wiltshire just as our son was going into the sixth form. He didn't like the idea of the move or the new school and he found it difficult to adjust to country living initially. However, most of the friends he now meets up with are the ones he made in that new life. He also grew to love the area we moved to, though we have now moved on to our second downshifting rural ideal (which he also loves!).

If you have only yourselves to consider then it's far easier. If one of you still needs to continue with their job but the other one is ready to go, then don't wait too long. Move to a location where commuting is still possible but you can also start enjoying that new life.

What I would say is that if you really are determined to take the step but are always putting it off until 'one day', don't wait any longer – life is too short to waste.

5. Are there added practical problems with moving between particular countries in the UK?

The short answer is, not really, although you should be aware that

Scotland has a different legal system from the rest of the UK, as well as a different educational system. So for a house move, the ideal is to move from Scotland to elsewhere in the UK; the most difficult house move is the other way round. If you are selling your house in Scotland and moving south of the border, then as soon as you accept an offer for your house (and any/all missives are dealt with), the transaction is legally binding. You then have a firm date on which you will receive the money and you are in a good position for buying that house in the south. If, however, you are selling property in England and buying in Scotland, you can never be sure of your southern sale until the contracts are exchanged. Meanwhile, if you have put in an offer for a property in Scotland and it has been accepted, you must come up with the money on the agreed date.

On the educational side of things, children move up to secondary education at the age of 12 in Scotland and 11 in the rest of the UK. The examination scene seems to be in a state of flux on both sides of the border, so it would be wise to make enquiries about the situation to any particular school you are interested in. In Scotland the education system sounds complicated but is very flexible in practice. Pupils usually sit the Standard Grade in the fourth year of secondary school. They then have the opportunity of going on to study for Highers. However, there are also the Intermediate 1 and 2 examinations. Intermediate 1 is usually for those who will not be going on to take the Higher in that subject and Intermediate 2, which is a little more advanced, is used either as a stepping stone for the Higher or as an alternative to the Higher in the subject. Additionally, there are the Advanced Highers. The advantage of all this diversity means that a course of examinations can be more or less tailormade for each child if the school has the facilities.

In the rest of the UK, pupils sit GCSEs at the age of 16, then A Levels two years later. AS Levels are equivalent to half an A Level in quantity (not quality) and are normally sat at the same time as A Levels, though it is sometimes possible to sit these after one year in the sixth form.

6. What do you find to do all day? Don't you get bored?

This is a question often asked by visitors. We have the cottage changeover day on a Saturday, but as for the rest of the week ... In fact, if we're thinking in business terms, then each week there is all the laundry to do, the book-keeping, the advertising, the website to keep up to date, the queries to answer and the bookings to take and to confirm. There are also the various maintenance jobs to do on the buildings and grounds, logs to gather and cut for the stoves and other physical work to keep the place in order.

However, if we are honest, this still leaves us with lots of free time. This is what we came here for! Because we are so isolated, I don't go into the shops very much. I've also lost my taste for city life. If the weather is good we take the opportunity to go for walks with the dogs or for a picnic in the glen. Any journey in the Highlands is through beautiful countryside, so is always a pleasure.

I've joined the local History Society and am a volunteer helper in the Visitor Centre in the village in the summer months. At present Chris is chairman of the committee which is organising the building of a new community centre. We belong to the Association of Scotland's Self Caterers and Chris is chairman of the Highland branch. He is also involved in a range of training and development activities and has a small flock of sheep and a working collie to play around with. With a widening range of activities and opportunities presenting themselves, he reckons he's beginning to 'upshift' again!

This still leaves us plenty of time to rush out and look at glorious sunsets or listen to the owls calling to each other on dark nights. We make time to stand in the courtyard and listen to the buzzards and their young above us in the pine forests and the red-throated divers out on the loch. Or on a lovely summer afternoon we might go down to the loch shore and just sit looking out over the water. Wonderful.

7. How do weekly budgets differ from when you were working conventionally?

Having a regular monthly salary meant that we could spend what we wanted to (within reason) in the sure knowledge that, come the end of the month, a further sum would be paid into the account. Now things are very different. There is no set sum appearing – the amount of money we have coming in fluctuates greatly. Even when bookings have been made and we know that money will be paid, we don't know exactly when. Bills have to be paid nevertheless and so we have to be careful.

Town living presents you with so much choice. Shops are full of tempting goods, supermarkets overflowing with produce. In our previous existence we used to buy all sorts of luxury food just when we felt like it. I didn't really have a set budget for food and going down to the cottage for the weekends meant we often did a second supermarket shop down in Wiltshire. Now we have to be circumspect. Our diet is much more down to earth, but I'm sure no less healthy. Our meals are certainly plainer and we rarely eat some of the more expensive foodstuffs. I enjoy cooking but my choice of menu is restricted now to those dishes without a long list of luxury ingredients.

We don't buy many new clothes. After all, we don't normally need office wear (apart from when Chris does development work on clients' premises), so both of us spend most of our days in comfortable clothes of the trousers, shirt and jersey variety.

If all this sounds gloomy to you, we don't find it so – some things simply don't matter so much.

8. Can you get the same level of service in the country (doctor/dentist/schools/library/transport)?

Transport is a real problem in country areas. Many villages have no bus service at all and a car is essential. Sometimes it's necessary to have two cars, especially if you live in a remote area. We're about seven miles from the nearest food shop and if one of us is away for the day or perhaps even two days, then the other would otherwise be completely stuck. It pays to be organized.

There is a medical practice in the next village, which is 14 miles from here. If it sounds a long way, it isn't. The roads are quiet and it takes less than 20 minutes. If we have an emergency then both the ambulance and the doctor can be here very quickly. Hospitals may be thin on the ground in the remote areas but then we don't usually have a long waiting time to be seen when we get there. We had a couple staying in one of the cottages recently when the wife became ill. Her husband took her into the local hospital where she was seen within 20 minutes and the staff apologized for the delay.

As her illness turned out to be serious, she was flown by helicopter to the hospital in Inverness. The couple were impressed with the level of service – it was the wife's first experience of flying. In their local city hospital they said they normally had to wait at least three hours to be seen.

Dentists are thin on the ground in the Highlands; there's a real shortage. In other areas you may find it just as much of a problem finding a dentist who will take National Health patients as in the towns. No better, no worse.

There is a primary school in the village with about 24 pupils. Local children are bussed to secondary schools either 7 (in one direction) or 26 miles away from the village.

I visit the library now and again, usually combining my visit with a shopping trip to the supermarket. You may also find that a library van will call in the village on a regular basis.

9. I've watched a few different TV programmes which follow people trying to downshift and relocate. How helpful and accurate do you think they are?

They're certainly interesting and they give some good reference points to look out for. It's always easier to spot mistakes and wrong-headedness in others, so these programmes are also valuable in letting you see the results of actions which you have probably identified as wrong. Just remember to use them as learning points when you are faced with similar decisions.

One thing they illustrate well is the comparative values of properties in different parts of the country. There used to be a belief that city property was much more expensive than rural property. This is true to a certain extent, especially if you are selling a property in London, but be realistic about property values. There have been examples of couples wanting to move from town to country while retaining a 'crash pad' in the town to allow one or both partners to continue in their current work, full or part time. As well as their choice of extensive country property invariably using up the majority of their available budget (and thus not leaving enough to buy the tiniest crash pad in town), the concept of trying to maintain both lives in parallel is not really what downshifting is about. If someone is initially trying to juggle two lives like this, we would probably advise keeping the town house and working life in the initial stages and weekending periodically down in the country, either by renting a self-catering property on a regular basis or buying a small property. We did this when we lived in London as our first practical realization of our downshifting/relocation plans (although not our first experience of living in the country). In Scotland, we have several guests who come quite regularly to 'their' cottage in our range of self-catering cottages, some of whom are getting a feel for the area with a view to downshifting ultimately.

Another fact that these programmes sometimes highlight is that small country properties don't appreciate in value to the same extent as many city properties. You therefore should not use the same arguments for justifying additional investment in refurbishment and extending your country property. With our first country cottage, when we still lived in London, we didn't make much, if any, profit when we sold it several years later (taking into account the costs of renovation and extension), but we had gained immense enjoyment from having our bolt hole in the country for weekends and holidays. There is, after all, more to life than property values.

Television programmes are also useful for giving you ideas of how to convert and renovate properties, for illustrating the structural problems to look out for and for highlighting the extent or lack of facilities which are available in particular locations. Some will show you the theories and realities of budgeting for the renovation work and how costs can easily spiral. It is also interesting to see the ever-increasing range of occupations which downshifters can adopt in a remote country location, thanks to technology and the 'electronic cottage' concept.

The different programmes have various angles on the range of considerations – the downshifting, the budgeting, the selection and detail of relocation, the changes in priorities and work/life balance. Some even offer a window onto how the project turned out when the programmes revisit former subjects. Watch and learn!

10. What happens if things begin to go wrong?

That depends very much on how honest you are with yourself and the tightness of grip that you have on your finances, business affairs and future marketing strategies. If your business planning has been realistic, you should be aware of your expected levels of income and expenditure and you should therefore resist the temptation to throw money at the problem if the money's not there. If your problems are financial, talk to people in the know – your bank or building society, for example – and try to sort out some form of consolidated solution. Harbour your finances and try to spend more wisely in the future.

If your problems are technical, bring in people who know the ins and outs of the technicalities. Sometimes (for things like private water supplies, for example) you're better finding the local guy who knows how things work in your area. At other times, when it's a high-tech problem and you're living in a rural location, you might have to bring in an expert from further afield in order to get a real solution, rather than some local guy who has never experienced the problem and attacks it by trial and error, progressively replacing parts (at your expense) to find the defective one.

If your problems are personal or social, such as not getting on with the locals, finding the reality of the location too remote or basic, or feeling that you and your partner are in each other's company too much, you need to sit down and talk through the problems and potential solutions. You may be able to do that yourself or you may need to involve the services of some form of counsellor. Don't let the situation drag on – confront it and come up with a viable solution.

In the longer term, things might begin to fade off, business wise. We've already discussed this in some detail under 'bell curve' in the previous chapter. The point to reiterate is that the possible decline is quite natural. Depending on your longer-term plans, you can respond to the decline in a variety of ways.

11. Where do we find out about all the ins and outs of setting up a business?

Your bank is a good starting point for information about setting up in business. It should have information leaflets on the subject. Better still, have a look at its website. Many have comprehensive guides to starting up and maintaining small businesses, with helpful hints as to where to start, where and how to get financial support, and exactly what to include in a business plan. Local enterprise councils are a good source of information too. They will often help with writing a business plan and with finding out about any grants available for your new business.

There are also the subsidies available for many rural properties and businesses. Try contacting the Rural Enterprise Scheme which aims to breathe life back into the countryside of England and Wales and may help you set up a small business. Or contact the Rural Development Service which pays grants for planting woodland. There is a publication available from Lloyds TSB which sets out all the subsidies and grants on offer from the various organizations. These may not all be business orientated but they may help you make your property work for you in other ways. Be warned though: the necessary red tape and business plans can be challenging and you will be ceding control to a certain extent. You will have to follow the rules laid down by the awarding of the grant – if you are claiming a subsidy for restoring farm buildings, for example, then the use of certain materials will be stipulated.

12. What are the key differences in moving from the town to the country?

Some of these are obvious, though perhaps not until you actually arrive in your new home. When we moved down to Wiltshire, our house was outside the village, down a country lane with no street lighting. We moved in winter and as the removal van left, it started to get dark. Unfortunately we hadn't noticed that there were hardly any central ceiling lights in the new house. We had to search the boxes frantically to find table lamps as the house grew darker and darker. Later that night, when I was alone in the house, the doorbell rang. As it was pitch black outside I must confess that I didn't dare answer the door. I later found out that a neighbour had called to welcome us to the village. The darkness can take you by surprise, but you quickly get used to it. It has a real plus side when you see the beauty of the sky on a starlit night – something you can never fully appreciate in a town.

Distances are greater in the country. But travelling to the supermarket through several miles of countryside is no burden – much more pleasurable than sitting in traffic in town. Visits to the cinema, to a restaurant or pub, to the theatre or to visit friends may take longer, or may not when you think of all the traffic you had to negotiate in the city. At least the journeys are more relaxing.

If you intend to carry on a business, you may have to be willing to travel, but if so, a wide range of wage-earning activities are possible. With the national network of flights growing year on year, it is becoming easier to travel around the country. Living up a small glen 50 miles south-west of Inverness, Chris can catch the early 'red eye' flight to Gatwick and be in a meeting in London by 10.00 am. He has to get out of bed around 04.30 in order to drive to the airport, so he wouldn't want to do it every day, but it does open up possibilities. He has run training events using video-conferencing facilities and provides coaching/mentoring services by e-mail and telephone link-ups, while obviously still travelling to provide some workshops and seminars face to face. The options are wide and varied but need not be too time consuming if scheduled sensibly to maintain that work/life balance.

As to life on a day-to-day basis, there are so many advantages to living in the country. Hanging out the washing on a frosty day, I once saw a fox lope unafraid over the fields behind the house. Watching from my sitting room windows I have seen the occasional deer walk along the road down at the lochside. The bird life is wonderful and we have an owl sitting in the rafters of the barn on many a night. If we travel a few miles westwards we can see the stags feeding at the roadside. You are much closer to nature and the seasons in the country – the first snow on the mountains, the sweep of the sun across the hillside and, of course, the west winds blowing fiercely in the winter months.

13. How can I turn a hobby into a living? How do I prepare?

In order to make a living, you need to be businesslike. You must sort out a business plan and have a clear idea of the services or products you are going to offer and how you are going to market and sell them. There's little point in building up large stocks of paintings, pottery pots or wooden carvings if nobody is buying them and you are therefore not receiving any income. If you think you're already proficient at producing the items to a professional standard, take objective opinion and advice on this from non-relatives, as there is some really amateurish tourist tat around on the shelves. You may decide that you could benefit from some more input, perhaps through a course or by speaking to other artists. Reach the point where you're proud of your product or service when you see it displayed side by side with the competition.

You don't necessarily have to extend a hobby directly or continue a previous profession or skill working from your home/office base. Sometimes a little lateral thinking is required.

- Interested in local history and keen on driving? Buy a people carrier and set up as a specific tour guide.
- A talented musician? Start a band and teach others to play.
- Interested in writing? Produce articles for publishing in local and national newspapers and magazines or find a publisher for your first novel.
- A natural cook? Open a small restaurant or offer your services to cook for private parties. Or extend it further and become a function organizer yourself.
- Like children? Set up a nursery, creche or babysitting service.

The list could go on and on. Don't settle for the first idea – think 'outside the box' a little. Check out what is already happening in your chosen area. Could you provide a better service or product? If you spot a gap in the market, could you fill it? What types of marketing are used in the area? Are you aware of any other ways to market which might catch the local eye as they are new and innovative?

The key question you need to ask yourself is: 'how am I going to market my service or product?' Finding an answer to this will help you refine exactly what your product or service should be and give you indicators of facilities and equipment which you will need in order to provide it. Objective discussions regarding expected quality standards, packaging and advertising will help to sharpen up your product or service and you will be well on your journey of change from hobbyist to professional.

14. How do I choose the correct level of downshifting?

This is obviously a personal question and answers will vary dramatically. I would really have to throw the question back to you to find out the most appropriate level. It depends on a range of considerations:

- the minimum income that you require;
- whether you want to focus on one activity or multi-task;
- how much free time you require for relaxation;
- whether you see this move as semi-retirement or a new business start-up;
- whether it's a shorter-term money spinner or a longer-term cash provider.

To combat the ups and downs of self-employment, it makes sense to build up a portfolio of interests – the multi-tasking referred to above. We referred earlier to the idea of flying kites, with some ideas lying dormant while others are active. This can of course create situations where you are perhaps busier than you intended being in your projected downshifted existence, but you can always motivate yourself through the knowledge that you are building up some financial reserves. These can then be used either to develop further business ideas or to support periods of non-work and relaxation.

In reality, you will probably find that you don't have total control over your level of downshifting, with markets, involvement and breadth of activity fluctuating quite dramatically over any given year. Working on the basis that you can always turn work down, or have a waiting list, it's better to have too much on the go rather than too little (which creates the financial pressures we have already considered extensively). For that reason, try to develop a portfolio of activities, even though you may have one main service or product which you wish to promote.

15. How do you sort out your work/life balance when you're self-employed?

This is a problem for many people, whether or not they are self-employed, have downshifted or have relocated to rural living. Work/

life balance involves more than just relative hours spent working; it also considers issues such as how you spend your waking hours overall and how you can blend life skills at work and vice versa.

It gets slightly more complicated when you are a self-employed sole trader as you are carrying all the responsibilities of the business on your shoulders. As you spend the majority of your time providing your chosen product(s) or service(s), the other secondary business activities such as administration, finance, advertising and marketing, procurement and distribution tend to be achieved in your 'spare time'. If you're working from a home base, it becomes very tempting to just pop back to the office in the evening to complete some of these secondary – but very important – activities. Doing this will obviously impact on your work/life balance.

Although there will naturally be crisis points when you will have to work longer hours to honour agreements and contracts, you must try as much as possible to establish normal working schedules which incorporate both primary and secondary elements of your business. This will provide the motivation to allow you to close the door and walk away from your business life in the evenings and weekends, as you would expect to do if you were an employee of a larger business.

Involved as you will be in virtually all aspects of your business, you should not experience the frustrations which you might face as an employee not being allowed to develop some of your latent skills. This is one of the additional aspects of normal work/life balance, in that you can meet the situation where someone gains experience applying skills in his life aspect because he is not being given scope to develop them at work. For example, someone who is prevented from being involved in giving training or business presentations at work could provide voluntary mentoring or business advice or get on the public speaking circuit. Alternatively, you can receive training and development in many soft skills at work which will help to improve your social skills in life generally. The same may be true for a sole trader. There is nothing to stop you booking up for further training and development. There are usually grants available to encourage you even further and much of the preliminary training at least can be achieved through e-learning, so you needn't even leave your desk!

16. Do you feel a loss of status when you downshift from a professional job?

You may – it's largely down to your attitude and how you view the situation. Gillean, for example, was a systems analyst, working for one of the major UK consultancy companies. Now she owns and manages a self-catering cottage business. The fact that she washes sheets, cleans bathrooms, handles telephone bookings and gets involved in the myriad (fairly mundane) tasks involved in the business does not detract from the fact that she owns a business and property worth thousands of pounds. And, as she has elaborated elsewhere, the quality of life is so much better than commuting to Reading.

Her ICT and business organizational experience has been of great value in developing our cottages business, which also provides additional job satisfaction and helps balance life and work. As I have detailed elsewhere, I am currently moving back into a greater involvement in training and development, but again focused on areas which are of particular interest to me. I too have parallel areas of involvement in the cottage business, including both the organization and the cleaning and preparation. We both enjoy writing, with our time spent on individual projects increasing year on year. So we see it more as a change of focus than a loss of status, but we do feel comfortable with our wide range of activities, which is evolving.

When we moved from London to Wiltshire, I downshifted fairly dramatically. Having cut back heavily on management development training and materials design, I became more involved in writing – and qualified as a massage therapist. As an off-shoot of this, I also manufactured and sold massage tables. This mixture of activities, in my experience, potentially created greater confusion than that experienced through 'loss of face'. One day I might be providing and delivering a training course which earned me several hundred pounds in fees; the next I might be giving two or three massages during the day, earning around £20 per hour. I might only have cleared around £80 per table, which took the best part of a day to produce. When you have varying hourly rate values bouncing around like that, it's difficult to equate values. You need to add the value of your personal enjoyment and satisfaction, plus the interest in developing a new venture, to gain some equation which gives your overall satisfaction rating.

You can extend this positive thinking even further to create the situation where you are involved in two or three high-earning days working at something which is perhaps more mundane or less satisfying, in order to subsidize your other days working on more enjoyable but less lucrative activities. The additional fact of having a range of wage-earning activities means that you are more likely to receive a reasonable income each month, even though the amounts will fluctuate. And when you've downshifted to rural living with simpler tastes and requirements, payments of £20 and £50 keep you going in groceries quite well! Life and its enjoyment are largely in your mind and heart and are truly of your making when you get your head round downshifting and relocation.

Onwards and upwards

There are doubtless many other questions which can and do crop up when we discuss such matters with individuals at meetings and in seminars. You could go on and on asking questions. We hope that by this stage, the detail in this book has given you enough confidence to reach your decisions, make your arrangements and set forth on your new path in life. In wishing you every encouragement and good wish, we would like to end with a final quotation, which brings all the thinking together wonderfully:

'Come to the edge,' he said.
They said, 'We are afraid.'
'Come to the edge,' he said.
They came.
He pushed them ... and they flew.
Guillaume Apollinaire

Appendix 1

Walking the talk

▥ Starting off

We began married life conventionally enough with both of us teaching in Scotland. At that time property was very inexpensive there and we bought our first house, a small stone cottage near Crieff in Perthshire, for very little. It had no heating except for an open fire in the sitting room. However, the cottage was so small that we managed to heat the whole house with this. The village was in the middle of some stunning scenery so we used to go for long walks with our first dog, a cairn terrier, whenever we could.

We spent three lovely years there, experiencing at first hand the joys and occasional tribulations of living in a small rural community. Then Chris decided that he wanted to specialize more in the technology side of education, lecturing in a London college, so, in location terms, we took the biggest leap possible from tiny hamlet to city life. I was expecting our first child at the time, so in many ways we were really making a break with the past and moving up the ladder.

We were lucky enough to be put in touch with the friend of a colleague who owned a flat in the Bayswater Road area of London. Chris, myself and Isla, the dog, moved in with this unsuspecting friend in early summer 1973.

While Chris went off to the college every morning, I scanned the papers for houses and travelled out to the suburbs to view properties. Things were getting pretty desperate by the time we saw the house we wanted and thought we could afford. Our daughter was born only a matter of three weeks after the move to Walton-on-Thames. We had picked a 1960s' semi-detached house with lots of light and space and it was a lovely change after the cottage with its small windows.

In those days there was not the same opportunity for childcare provision and anyway, I had always assumed that I would be staying at home to look after our daughter. Unfortunately, in our inexperience, we had let our enthusiasm for the house override our financial judgement and it came to a point after one academic year where we just couldn't afford to live there any longer. Anywhere in the London area would be difficult, we realized, even in those days, and travelling was expensive.

▪ The middle years

Our next move involved a return to Scotland where Chris worked as an Educational Technology Advisor in a national centre in Glasgow. Houses were cheaper in the north and we found a modern detached house in Helensburgh, on the west coast, amid fantastic scenery. There was a big downside to this area though, as we found out very quickly. I don't know whether the winter of 1974 was a particularly wet one, but according to my calculations, there were only ten days between October and March when it was completely dry. It was all very depressing, especially as the views from the house over the River Clyde were amazing, especially at night when the lights across the water made it feel more like Monte Carlo (albeit in the rain!).

This, coupled with untenable working conditions, encouraged us to move once again quite rapidly, this time to the far south of England, near Portsmouth. Our son was born there so I still wasn't working. Chris was by now the manager responsible for relocating and developing an in-service development and resource centre in the city and really enjoyed the work. It took very little time travelling to and from work so we had lots of time together with the children. We spent three years there and made some close friends.

We grew to love the Hampshire countryside, visiting pubs at the weekends and on summer nights. It was a good life, with a mixture of rural and city living, and it proved quite possible to enjoy it on only one salary.

Then, with the centre up and running and the challenge and new experiences diminishing, we grew restless again. Chris wanted to move into business training to a greater extent and took a post as a consultant with a business training consultancy, again located in London. This relatively rapid succession of moves between Scotland and England and rural and urban living proved to be a valuable learning experience in terms of relocation, with all the associated legal, financial and social implications.

My mother nobly came down to our home near Portsmouth to look after the children while we travelled up to London looking for somewhere to live. We didn't have anywhere particular in mind so spent time driving round the suburbs comparing areas. We loved Chiswick, Kew and Richmond but didn't see how we could afford a house in any of them. We persisted, however, and at last struck gold.

An estate agent told us of a property coming on to the market in Richmond. It was in pretty bad shape as it had been neglected for a number of years. Two recluses had lived there, one upstairs and one down, and because of its condition it would be on the market at a reasonable price. It was our chance and we took it.

We moved in two weeks before Christmas. My long suffering mother came for the holiday and my abiding memory of her visit was hearing her cry of surprise on Christmas morning. "Look, there's snow inside my window!" And there was.

We had to install damp proofing, central heating, a new plumbing system and bathroom and downstairs loo. All this went on while we lived in the house with only two gas fires for warmth. The children were then aged five and two and were no trouble at all. They took it all in their stride – riding their bike and tractor through the hall and kitchen and playing games upstairs when all the floorboards were up downstairs.

We had many wonderful years living in Richmond. We loved the restaurants, bars, shops and, of course, the river. We had lots of visitors too, relations and friends coming to see us and to see London. Both children were now at school and I was thinking about going back to teaching again. I took a job at a secondary school in Wimbledon, filling in for teachers on maternity leave. It was great to have two salaries again, especially as there was still work we wanted to do on the house.

▓ Living abroad

Then Chris saw an advertisement for a job in Brussels – International Training Manager for an American company. It sounded marvellous and promised to be for a number of years – an important factor as we still had a by now fairly aged Isla and did not want to put her into quarantine by coming home early.

Brussels was a great adventure and both children loved it. They went to the British school there and made friends from all over the globe. At weekends we travelled to Holland, Germany, France or Switzerland. It was a wonderful opportunity.

The house in Brussels was rented as we had kept our London house, putting it in the hands of a rental agency. We weren't too impressed with the service they provided but there were no disasters at least. At one stage we had the tenants of the house phoning us and holding the telephone close to the boiler to demonstrate the 'funny' noise the boiler was making. As Chris visited Britain regularly on business, he managed to keep an eye on things and maintain direct relations with our tenants.

All this came to an end sooner than we expected. The parent company decided to close the office in Brussels and we were soon home again – with the poor dog in six months' quarantine at the age of 14.

▓ Home again

After a brief period as a consultant with a computer-based training company, Chris decided to strike out on his own, cushioned with a redundancy payment from the American company. We set up an office in one of the bedrooms and he worked from home. Disillusioned with teaching, I decided to train as a systems analyst and joined the Civil Service. I loved the work and it was wonderful not having all the marking and preparation in the evenings. Chris, meanwhile, was building up a client base of business companies, providing a range of training services including consultancy, multimedia and open learning material design and production as well as the delivery of customised management development training courses.

After a few years with the Treasury, I joined the Stock Exchange, travelling to the city every day for five years. It was relatively easy from Richmond but I hated the last part, the Waterloo and City line – it was always packed with commuters.

Life went on smoothly until gradually we began to be aware of the increasing traffic and crowds in London. The houses in the road we lived in, previously inhabited by single people or elderly ladies, were all being sold to young couples with two or more cars. At the weekends it got to the stage where we thought twice about taking the car anywhere because it would be impossible to park when we got back.

We began to dream about that cottage in the country. My mother had by this time moved to Salisbury. In visiting her at weekends we grew to love the Wiltshire countryside – the chalk streams around Salisbury and the open downland in the north. With the help of a small legacy, we found a compact cottage in Urchfont, outside Devizes. It faced the duck pond and an open green. There was a lot of work to be done on it but we could see the potential. Once the builders had finished the extension and renovation, we spent as much time there as we could. By now, though, the children had grown and didn't want to leave London at the weekends. They saw no benefit in the country at all so we had to compromise, spending some weekends away and some at home.

At last we couldn't stand it any longer. No amount of restaurants, bars, theatres and shops could make up for the packed streets, the crowded underground and the traffic. In fact, having gone to the ballet one evening in London, it took us two hours to get home by tube and bus. Definitely not worth it.

Our daughter was starting university and our son was just going into the sixth form at school. If we didn't move then we would have to wait for another two years. We took the chance. I handed in my notice. Chris could potentially provide the same client-based service from any location, although (rather unfortunately for us) several of his major clients had fallen by the wayside around the time of our move, due to massive reorganizations, takeovers and in one case receivership. This did little to colour our future cash-flow projections but the sale value of our London property after appreciation over 14 years had left us reasonably cash-rich. We had been looking for houses on an ongoing basis for a number of months but nothing had materialized. So we packed up all our belongings and furniture, put most of it in store and moved into the cottage. Our son went to a school in a nearby village and hated it. They didn't play football there, only rugby.

We looked around the area at every available house and at last found one we liked. It was larger than we had planned but it had the right number of bedrooms and a lovely garden. It stood among fields on the edge of a small village outside Pewsey. Chris had been reading up about old timber-framed buildings and this was one *par excellence*. It was also thatched, something we really didn't want, but we had looked at so many houses without success that we decided to go ahead.

The cottage by the green in Urchfont had been in the centre of a village with street lighting. This property – a sixteenth-century manor house – was almost on its own and pitch black at night. It took a little adjustment on our part, helped by the addition of some external floodlighting. It was also glorious to have so much countryside around us and the peace and quiet was just what we had wanted. People in the village were friendly and we were made welcome. There was even a cottage in the garden – an amazing bonus – and this we renovated and started to develop as a holiday letting business.

Having downshifted as I thought, I had a call from the Stock Exchange asking me to go back to work for them on a contract basis. The offer was too good to miss but I certainly didn't want to travel into London on a daily basis. After all, that's what I was hoping to get away from. So a compromise was reached. I would travel in for three days a week and work at home for the rest. From our local station it was a journey of under an hour to London. The trains at that time were quiet and mostly on time. Chris would take me to the station, walk the dog and be at his desk in the office in the house by nine o'clock. As well as continuing with some training consultancy work, he too had decided to downshift, spending more of his time writing professional articles and a book, as well as a novel.

I was glad when it all ended after two years as the travelling was taking its toll. The long-distance trains were good but the underground was pretty unpleasant. I found the working from home a great idea. I didn't have to dress up and could be at my desk very early. It was hard to switch off though and I had to force myself sometimes not to go back in the evenings to do that little bit more.

The house was costing us quite a bit – the thatch was on a rolling maintenance programme. Heating bills were high too as there was no insulation in the walls and in some cases we could see gaps between the timbers and the infill. The sitting room chimney was a huge inglenook and you could stand in it and see the stars. But at least our son had settled into the area. He often had friends staying overnight and we would come down in the mornings to bodies, wrapped in duvets, lying all over the place. He bought a very old car and was able to be more independent.

I found work with a computer consultancy. This meant a bit of travelling but not as much as before. It was bearable and meant we could still live as we wanted. By now, Chris's clients had tailed off and our son was going off to university. Having developed an interest in holistic living and thinking, Chris was working on a model for applying this within business, using skills such as internal mentoring, self-empowerment and relaxation techniques. To this end, he qualified as a massage therapist, adding this to his 'basket' of income-earning activities.

Another sea change

We had really started to rethink our lives again. We needed a new focus. Did I want to go on working as I was? Should we think about a completely different lifestyle? Did this mean another house move? We still wanted to be country based. There was no way we were going back to town living. We loved Wiltshire and might have been happy staying there, but an even more remote countryside was calling us.

We tried to think of a way of earning income while still enabling us to spend time together and more time at home. Self-catering seemed the answer. We had got used to letting out the cottage and it had proved to be a relatively successful enterprise. For us the idea had many advantages over offering guest house accommodation and meant that we could still have that precious privacy within our own home.

We started to look at estate agents' leaflets and websites. We needed somewhere large enough to have three cottages at least, to be economically viable, plus our own house. Perhaps somewhere with outbuildings for conversion would be a possibility. As we were more interested in the prospect of traditional buildings, we established early on that the potential for buying an existing chalet park type of business was not for us. We tried Dorset, Somerset, Wiltshire and Hampshire without any luck – all the properties we saw in the south of England were too expensive.

▪ The answer

We had seen the BBC programmes *Wilderness Walks* based on mountain walks in the more remote areas of the UK. On a holiday that year in the Western Highlands of Scotland we decided to try one of these walks in an area known as the last wilderness in Britain – Knoydart. Driving along the single track road to Kinlochourn to begin our walk, we saw a small hotel up on the right-hand side of the road looking down over the loch and the mountains. It was love at first sight and, in that moment, I knew that I wanted to live there. We went on to the end of the road and carried on with our intended walk. We had an ancient (and heavy) tent with us and food for two days. We intended to camp at Barrisdale Bay and then walk over the mountains to Inverie the following day. Alas the spirit was willing but the body was weak! We camped for the night just as the programme suggested but were driven mad by the midges and kept awake by a generator in a stalker's house which went on until late and started early the next day.

The walk was abandoned and we resolved to try to stop over the following night in the hotel we had spotted. Alas it was full, but we were even more enchanted by what we could see of the inside of the building. The one drawback of course was that it was not for sale.

Trying to be logical about our plan, we circulated our requirements to all the major Scottish agents, asking for details of any properties that might be suitable throughout the Highlands, realizing that we could probably afford something of the right size there. There were surprisingly few suitable houses. We wanted a house that extended in a linear way rather than a tall building with several storeys. This would make it easier to convert into cottages, each with its own front door.

As we drew up a shortlist of all the points we were looking for in our ideal property, we realized that the hotel we had seen fulfilled all of them. It became our benchmark.

We did go to see some properties but somehow they were never quite perfect. One very grand house in Perthshire was in shadow all winter, the sun never rising above the opposite hill until the summer months. Another house looked suitable on paper. Unfortunately, there was a hotel further up the same road with about 40 self-catering chalets – competition on a grand scale.

We went to stay at the hotel we had seen on our walk. We stayed there several times, on each occasion asking for a different bedroom in order to check out the layouts and scope for conversion. We took photographs of each other standing outside the hotel in different areas. The more we saw, the more we loved it and the more perfect it seemed for our purpose. Its advantages were obvious – a cobbled courtyard with the building round it, enough bedrooms for three cottages and a house, outbuildings, a stone barn. Our investigations had convinced us that the hotel would be relatively easily separated into cottages and a home for us, with unusually large windows looking south over a breathtaking view and beautifully proportioned rooms.

Disadvantages seemed few – we wondered whether it was too far north, too remote for visitors. It was off the main road: would we be snowed in during the winter months?

It was a long drawn-out process, over more than two years, to progressively float the possibility and then negotiate with the owners towards their agreeing to sell. Having managed to gain healthily from selling the old manor house, we could afford to make the proverbial 'offer which couldn't be refused'. At last the house was ours and we could begin the grand plan.

■ Self-catering in the Highlands

We moved in to Ardochy in October and assumed that we would have the building converted and be up and running by the following spring. Not so. Before buying the property we had of course checked with the planning authorities whether our application for change of use and the building conversion work would be looked on favourably. The planners were happy with the idea in principle but couldn't accept a planning application until the house was ours.

There were no real difficulties, but the whole process took much longer than expected. It was underlined that, in this west coast area, it was necessary for an architect to draw up plans and present the application. Having followed the ground rules, the process went ahead smoothly. However, with this and the building warrants, work wasn't able to start for quite a while. Part of the building was already a separate cottage so, by installing oil-fired central heating and redecorating, we had managed to get this one up and running in time for the millennium. However, by the time the refurbishment and building work had been completed on the other two cottages to the point that they were ready for letting, it was September and the summer letting season was drawing to a close. By the following spring we were very much in need of some serious income. Unfortunately that was the year of the foot and mouth epidemic. Though there were no cases in the Highlands, we had sheep on our land and had to take precautions. We remained closed until after Easter.

After this somewhat inauspicious start to our new venture, things could only get better. And they did. We are happily established as a business now, with a large percentage of repeat visitors. Chris and I are both involved in writing, with Chris also facilitating a variety of training and development work, both locally and with clients nationally – although controlled in order to spend the majority of his time at home. We love the life here, and although there are days that we are very busy with the business, if the sun is shining and the sky is blue, we take time off to enjoy the wonderful hills and glens of the Western Highlands – this is, after all, why we came here, and this is why we'll stay.

Appendix 2
Useful reference sources

Planning and setting up your business

Some of the major banks offer excellent advice on their websites for planning and setting up a small business.

www.bankofscotland.co.uk/business/startup
www.ukbusiness.hsbc.com
www.natwest.com/smallbusinesses

Business Gateway

A service provided by the Scottish Enterprise Network and its partners to give a single access point for integrated services for businesses in Scotland. This is also useful for running a business.

www.bgateway.com

Local Investment Networking Company

An independent non-profit-making organization acting as the National Business Angel Network for Scotland. These are people who choose to invest money in new companies and provide advice.

www.linscot.co.uk

Local Enterprise Agencies

www.scottish-enterprise.com

▪ Running a business

Chambers of Commerce

www.chamberonline.co.uk

Business Link

Practical help and advice for small businesses.

www.businesslink.gov.uk

▪ Training you and your staff

Learning and Skills Councils in England and Wales

www.lsc.gov.uk

Scottish Enterprise Network

www.scottish-enterprise.com

Self-development

The Integrated Triangle (business model for applying self-development with associated personal planning system).

www.the-integrated-triangle.com

Finding small businesses in the country

The Business Partnership

www.business-partnership.com

Nationwide Businesses

www.BusinessesForSale.com

Christie

www.christie.com

Bradford and Bingley

www.marketplace.co.uk

Accounting software packages

MYOB (Mind Your Own Business)

Software designed for small businesses. First Accounts package for start-ups and self-employed.

www.myob.co.uk

Simply Books

Easy-to-use package for very small businesses and small traders.

www.simplybooks.net

Grants

Small Business Services' R & D Project Grant Scheme

www.businesslink.gov.uk

Local Development Agencies and Councils

www.grantnet.com

Moving house

Online estate agency directory

www.House-Moving.co.uk

Any estate agent's website but also:
www.findaproperty.com
www.RightSearch.co.uk

Finding out about local house prices in Scotland

www.myhouseprice.com

Index

Aga/Rayburn, 52
architects, 81
arts workshops, 47, 48

bell curve, 124
  entrepreneur use, 124, 125
  long term application, 125
  'cash cow' use, 125, 126
big picture thinking, 26
blue waters, 27
book-keeping, 114–116
budgeting, 6, 7, 123, 124, 132, 133
building
  change of use, 82
  costs, 121, 122
  work, 80
buying property
  England and Wales, 82, 83
  Scotland, 83–85, 130, 131
  Scottish 'offer' system, 84, 85
business
  options, 18, 25, 26, 139
  plans, 6, 108–112, 138, 139

start-up, 120, 129, 136, 137, 138, 139

cash books, 115, 116
cash flow, 112–114
checking areas, 5
coastal options, 35
consolidation, 73, 74
contingency fund, 81, 121

darkness, 71, 137
dentists and doctors, 133, 134
downshifting, 3, 5, 11–13, 29, 66, 72, 73, 128, 129, 130, 140, 142
driveway maintenance, 105

educational systems, 131
electricity
  consumer units, 104
  rural, 103, 104

family decisions, 22
farming, 36, 49, 129, 130

fencing, 106, 107
filling the day, 131, 132
financial
    considerations, 69–71, 124–126,
        142, 143
    forecasting, 111, 118, 119
flexible choice, 61, 62

geographic options, 33–35
grants, 85, 86, 141

heating systems, 100, 101
hotels, guest houses, B & Bs, 43–45
house with office, 50

inspiration, 68, 143
integration, 127, 128
island options, 40

kite flying, 58, 59

land ownership, 105–107, 129, 130
life change, 18
lifestyle, 4
local suppliers, 95, 96
loss of status, 142, 143

market gardens, 49
marketing, 60, 61, 109, 110, 122,
        123, 138, 139
money
    matters, 118
    planning, 118, 119
    setting up, 120, 121
    refurbishment, 121, 122
    first year, 122, 123
    longer term, 123, 124
mountain and moorland, 39
multi-tasking, 70, 96, 140

networking, 95, 96, 104, 105, 123,
        127, 128, 136

office technology, 94, 95
outdoor centres, 49, 50

paperwork, 91, 92, 122
personal
    development, 143
    organisation, 91, 92
    profiling, 11, 14–17, 66, 110
planning, 7, 128, 129
planning permission, 80
prioritising, 19, 20
project management, 81, 121,
        122
property, 4, 51
    checklist, 51
    considerations, 52, 98, 99
    costs, 80, 81
    sourcing, 79
    surveys, 78
    valuation, 77, 78

relocation, 3, 71, 72, 99, 100, 119
room layouts, 90, 91
rural living, 39, 103, 104
rural services, 133, 134

self catering, 46, 47
self employment, 57, 58, 62, 141
self sufficiency, 129, 130
septic tanks, 53, 101, 102
shop and gallery, 48
small community living, 38
solitude, 72
stables, 49
SWOT analysis, 23–25, 28, 67, 68

television, 1, 134, 135
time for change, 130
time management, 59, 60, 92, 93,
        131, 132, 141
town and city options, 36
transport, 41, 42
travel, 137, 138
trouble shooting, 135, 136

village options, 37

water supply, 53, 102, 103

work
  scheduling, 92, 93
  space design, 90, 91
  space in the home, 89, 90

working day, 92, 93
working from home, 88, 89
work/life balance, 2, 5, 55, 56, 63,
  64, 74, 93, 94, 140, 141

2727402R00093

Printed in Great Britain
by Amazon.co.uk, Ltd.,
Marston Gate.